MUSIC THERAPY
IN PRINCIPLE
AND PRACTICE

ABOUT THE AUTHORS

Donald E. Michel, Ph.D., LPC, Emeritus Professor, Texas Woman's University. Known as a pioneer in the field of music therapy, he established one of the first music therapy programs in the country at the Veterans Hospital in Topeka, Kansas, upon his return from Naval service in World War II. He also established the first music therapy internship with the University of Kansas. In 1954, he established the academic program in music therapy at Florida State University, which he directed until 1975, when he became coordinator of the music therapy program at Texas Woman's University until his retirement in 1992. Working in the field (part-time for TWU for five years after retirement), he continues to learn through research and writing in his lifelong profession. He is also a Licensed Professional Counselor (LPC) as well as was one of the first Registered Music Therapists. His honors include President (1959–61), Honorary Life Member, and recipient of the Presidential Citation for Lifetime Achievement of the National Association for Music Therapy (NAMT, now AMTA), Distinguished Alumnus at Missouri Western College, and Life Honorary Member of the Southwestern Region of AMTA. He is known for his extensive research and publications in the field and has traveled the world as a lecturer and workshop leader. He is life member Phi Mu Alpha Sinfonia, Phi Kappa Phi, and Rotary International. He takes pride in his family, spouse, two children, and four grandchildren.

Joseph Pinson, M.A., MT-BC is a member of the faculty at Texas Woman's University, where he teaches courses in music therapy. Mr. Pinson holds degrees in music from Southern Methodist University and the American University and all level certification in music education in the State of Texas. From 1974 until 1997, he was Director of Music at Denton State School, a residential facility for persons with developmental disabilities. He is director of the Denton Bell Band, the Denton Senior Center Chime Choir, and the Redbud Ringers. He is a published composer and has received the annual ASCAP Standard Award since 2000. He is a former member of the Board of the American Guild of English Handbell Ringers and former President and Honorary Life Member of the Southwestern Region of the American Music Therapy Association.

MUSIC THERAPY IN PRINCIPLE AND PRACTICE

By

DONALD E. MICHEL, Ph.D., LPC

and

JOSEPH PINSON, M.A., MT-BC

CHARLES C THOMAS • PUBLISHER, LTD.
Springfield • Illinois • U.S.A.

Published and Distributed Throughout the World by

CHARLES C THOMAS • PUBLISHER, LTD.
2600 South First Street
Springfield, Illinois 62704

©2005 by CHARLES C THOMAS • PUBLISHER, LTD.

ISBN 0-398-07542-5 (hard)
ISBN 0-398-07543-3 (paper)

Library of Congress Catalog Card Number: 2004053734

With THOMAS BOOKS *careful attention is given to all details of manufacturing
and design. It is the Publisher's desire to present books that are satisfactory as to their
physical qualities and artistic possibilities and appropriate for their particular use.*
THOMAS BOOKS *will be true to those laws of quality that assure a good name
and good will.*

Printed in the United States of America
GS-R-3

Library of Congress Cataloging-in-Publication Data

Michel, Donald E.
   Music therapy in principle and practice / by Donald E. Michel and Joseph Pinson.
      p. cm.
   Includes bibliographical references and index.
   ISBN 0-398-07542-5 – ISBN 0-398-07543-3 (pbk.)
      1. Music therapy. I. Pinson, Joe. II. Title.

ML3920/M483 2004
615.8'5154–dc22

                                                          2004053734

PREFACE

For many years *Music Therapy* (Michel, D., 1976, 1985) has been a standard textbook at many universities. During discussions with Joseph Pinson about a third edition, it was decided to create a new textbook, one which presents music therapy from the perspective of Michel's fifty-plus years as an educator, clinician, and researcher and Pinson's thirty-plus years as a clinician, educator, and composer. *Music Therapy in Principle and Practice* offers the student or anyone interested in learning about the profession an overview from two important perspectives–combining valuable information from research as a basis for principles with the realities of hands-on experience as a basis for practice.

This book approaches therapy from the position of assessing developmental skills in individuals served. We include a good amount of information regarding diagnosis; however, it is our opinion that the focus of treatment should be based upon the needs (for habilitation and/or rehabilitation) that are apparent at the time of assessment. We encourage each therapist and each person reading this book to be aware of levels of stress–before, during, and following treatment. These may be the key to improvement and maintenance of the condition that is the focus of treatment. The ability to manage or cope with the anxiety associated with any life situation is very important, especially if the condition is one that is likely to present during the entire life of the individual.

A glance at the Contents of this book reveals that beyond the basic principles and mechanics of assessment and protocol planning, we have discussed treatment of various types of lifetime developmental skills. Each of these is further explored with regard to different populations served and the various strategies that have been found to be effective. There is a very strong chapter dealing with professional ethics, because we feel that the quality of treatment that is possible and the stability and reputation of our association hinges on these principles.

Donald E. Michel
Joseph Pinson

CONTENTS

MUSIC THERAPY
IN PRINCIPLE
AND PRACTICE

Chapter 1

THE FIELD OF MUSIC THERAPY

- Defining Music Therapy
- Basic Philosophical Concepts
- Historical Perspectives
- Employment Opportunities

DEFINING MUSIC THERAPY

One of the earliest philosophical pioneers, E. Thayer Gaston, seemed to avoid a specific definition. In *Music in Therapy* (1968), he chose to discuss rather than define. Gaston saw that music was a stimulus, which trained therapists could utilize to elicit certain measurable responses (relaxation, arousal, associations, etc.) in therapy. The title of the book suggests that music is the principal agent of change. Many of the ideas expressed in this book have had great influence on subsequent publications. In one of the chapters of *Music in Therapy*, Sears (1968) defined or described the profession in terms of its processes (based upon work of several clinicians).

It is important to understand the difference between so-called "**therapeutic music**" and music therapy. The former describes a relationship between an individual and his/her music. In one instance, a person may relax by listening to favorite recordings, or in another, rhythmic music may provide a motivating background for exercise. Neither of these is necessarily part of a prescribed regimen that includes personal interaction with a professional music therapist, which is an important element of **music therapy**.

In the relationship between the individual and music, the person involved could either be listening to a performance (recorded or live) or he/she could be performing the music. Usually a higher level of involvement is achieved through listening to live music, and an even higher level in performance.

Music therapy is a relationship among all three–the individual, the therapist, and the music. For the purposes of therapy, neither listening nor performance alone achieves the level of **structure** and **interaction**, which is inherent in the triangle shown in Figure 1. Other variations of this process may occur with group activities; however, the relationship between the therapist and the individual is of primary importance, as in other health professions. The triangle, suggested in a conversation with a former student, Rae Sirott, illustrates the dynamics of this relationship.

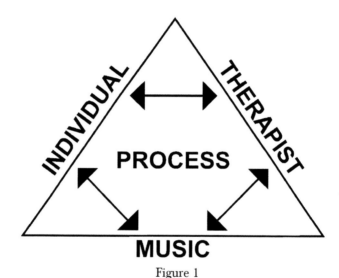

Figure 1

Just as the triangle in the illustration is a *stable* device of construction, the combination of elements in the therapeutic equation provides stability and structure. Music is a "common ground of sound" (Pinson, 1989) on which the needs of all participants may be met in an effective and efficient manner.

For many years music therapists have debated which is most important–the music itself, or the relationship between therapist and the individual served. There are good arguments for either interpretation.

Another consideration is that music may be thought of as a continuum within the structure of a single piece or as it is used throughout a treatment process. At any moment within a performance or a listening experience, the emphasis may shift from the music to the relationship and vice-versa. If we place music (represented by a solid line) and the relationship (represented by a broken line) on the same time path (moving from left to right), their importance at any given moment may be quite different and at times (where the lines cross), the same (Figure 2).

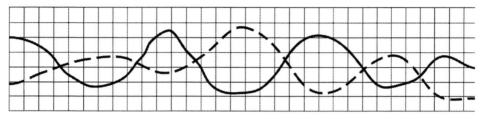

Figure 2

In the fields of therapy and medicine, it is not a simple task to find a definition that applies to all situations. The purpose of this discussion is to get the reader started toward developing his/her own definition of music therapy—one that is flexible enough to be applied to most situations. One useful exercise may be to define both music and therapy individually to better understand the basic elements of a definition.

The section that follows is very much like a conversation between the authors. To make yourself a part of the conversation, you may want to add your own "and furthermore" between the paragraphs.

Music Defined (Michel, 1985)

Music is human behavior, and as such it can be thought of as various skills such as vocalizing or producing sounds in organized patterns which can be measured.

Music differs from other forms of organized sound, such as speech. Words are sometimes incorporated, but music also has a strong nonverbal content which allows expression of feelings symbolically.

And Furthermore (Pinson)

The behavior of making music includes all life skills. Even when one makes music alone, most of these skills come into play. These are different in each individual.

The symbolic associations that individuals experience in music are influenced by differences in cultural background, listening experiences, and intelligence. Music also uses a greater variety of frequencies than those found in speech.

In all societies where history has been recorded, there has been evidence of some system of sound that has been called music. For sound to be called music, more than one person should agree on such a definition.

It is conceivable that one individual, isolated from all human contact, might produce unique sounds, which were a satisfying experience and might be called music by that person in the absence of anyone who might disagree.

Generally, music is perceived as a pleasurable activity, and thereby may serve as reward or reinforcement in therapeutic use.

This pleasurable aspect of music makes it very valuable, especially in situations where building self-esteem is important to the outcome of the therapeutic process.

Music is usually produced within quite precise time boundaries, and this makes it very useful as a medium for structuring activities, especially those related to learning.

The timed responses inherent in music provide a framework for creativity and for the expression of ideas; and their "here and now" existence is a strong **metaphor** for the common experiences of everyday life.

Therapy Defined (Michel)

The dictionary defines "therapy" as ". . . remedial treatment of a bodily disorder . . . (or) . . . psychotherapy (as) an agency designed to bring about social adjustment" (Glanze, 1983).

And Furthermore (Pinson)

Neither definition speaks to the *personal* interaction between therapist and client, which, in many instances, is the critical factor that determines the success or failure of the therapeutic process.

Masserman (1966) finds in the root of the word "therapy" the meaning of "service," and states that ". . . serving the best interests of a fellow human being . . . is the purpose of all treatment as well as the hallmark of civilization."

In that music therapy is based around mostly constructive (usually enjoyable) activity, it may be more difficult for some to see it as "service." Those who experience the positive effects of music therapy know that they have been "served" in a grand way.

Almost anything done for people in need, or anything they do for themselves may be called *therapy*; however, when professionals use the term, it usually has a more definite connotation that includes specific measures aimed at - improvement of/for specific problems.

Playing your CD's may be in some way *therapeutic*, but such activity could be called therapy only if it were part of a planned program of intervention. Even active participation in music making would need measurable outcomes for it to be defined as *therapy*.

An implied meaning of therapy is change—from an undesirable condition to a more desirable one. In this sense, therapy has a similar definition to that of learning, i.e., "changed behavior." Modern concepts of therapy very closely relate, and sometimes equate therapy and learning.

Changes in the educational progress of normal individuals often take place at a rapid rate that is measurable. The changes that occur in the therapeutic process, especially with persons with severe developmental delay, as well as those with psychological problems, often take place at a slow rate that is more difficult to measure.

Masserman (1966) states that therapy in the psychological sense is ". . . the science, techniques, and art of exerting a favorable influence on behavior disorders by every ethical means available," and defines psychotherapy as ". . . the science and art of influencing behavior so as to make it (a) more compatible with social norms and (b) more efficient and satisfactory to the individual."

Music provides one of the most ethical, acceptable, universal, efficient, and satisfactory approaches to behavior disorders, because the focus is set in a medium that is potentially friendly, non-threatening, uplifting, and time-oriented. Music exists in the present tense, and, therefore, many of the successes that individuals experience in music may apply directly to everyday functioning.

Further Definitions

When music, as an agent of change, is used to establish a therapeutic relationship, to nurture a person's growth and development, to assist in self-actualization, the process is music therapy.

Edith Boxill (1985)

Music therapy is a systematic process of intervention wherein the therapist helps the client to achieve health, using music experiences and the relationships that develop through them as dynamic forces of change.

Kenneth Bruscia (1989)

Music therapy is the application of treatment procedures or protocols which are individualized and use what is culturally and individually recognized as music to achieve, along with the therapist's contribution to a "therapeutic relationship," certain goals, pre- and continuously determined by assessment of the needs of the individual.

Donald Michel

Music therapy is the treatment of the total individual through planned personal interaction and continuous manipulation of the musical environment.

Joseph Pinson

What Is NOT Music Therapy

Since music has been defined as being culturally determined organized sound patterns, and since therapy has been defined as individualized treatment based upon a person's needs and often a unique relationship between therapist and client, procedures which do not meet these criteria are NOT music therapy.

Professional music therapists are those persons who earn that designation because of their **specialized education**, both in the classroom and in the clinic. This training has been prescribed by an authorized organization, the American Music Therapy Association, which operates within guidelines established by recognized medical and health authorities. Those who call themselves music therapists, but who are not qualified as stated, fall into the category of "pseudo," non-professional, or self-proclaimed "practitioners."

BASIC PHILOSOPHICAL CONCEPTS

The Music Therapist's Creed—*Donald Michel*

I believe in music therapy, because I believe in music as an effective, communicative, therapeutic tool, and as an important and necessary part of many persons' lives. I believe in music therapy, because I believe in therapy—that is, I believe that persons in distress can and should be helped. I believe in music therapy that is based upon scientific theory and research, because it is a most accountable, ethical, and helpful therapy for those who need it. I believe in music therapy, because I believe that the "essence of life" is in what contributions one can make to it, and that my chosen profession provides me with a unique and wonderful means for making such contributions. (Michel, 1962, rev. 2003)

Music Therapy Philosophy—*Joseph Pinson*

Treatment provided by a trained therapist, who understands that his/her contribution is in most instances critical to success, is based upon the knowledge that music, with its unique qualities of melody, rhythm, and harmony, is an effective tool to facilitate change in various behaviors. Music therapy may be effective to some degree with any person, regardless of age, disability, or musical background; however, it is most effective with persons who have music skills and/or an affinity for the medium. Since music is essentially a form of nonverbal communication, it may benefit those who are less responsive to other therapies. (revised, 2003)

The two statements on the philosophy of music therapy above, which have been developed from the experience of the authors, provide a basis for our discussion. It is as important to know why we do what we do as it is to know how to do it. The interaction between persons in many therapeutic relationships is very intense, and the therapist who enters this arena with any motives other than to help the individual in need is laying the groundwork for frustration and possible failure.

The statements of the authors have these things in common: (1) Both recognize music as an effective therapeutic tool. (2) Both recognize music as a medium of communication. (3) Both recognize that the contribution of the therapist is important. (4) Both recognize the "universal" nature of this therapy.

Whereas Michel describes music as "an important and necessary part of many persons' lives," Pinson feels that music therapy is "most effective with persons who have music skills and/or an affinity for the medium." Both are personal opinions that are not yet supported by research.

Michel speaks of the rewards of his chosen profession, which "provides me with an unique and wonderful means for making such contributions," and, although not stated in his music therapy philosophy, Pinson feels that, as a clinician, he has always *received* more than he has ever been able to give.

Neither of the philosophical positions states exactly how music therapy fits into the larger context of medicine and general health. How we function as therapists is influenced by how we view health and illness in general. Just as music therapy has been defined as an ***individualized*** process, the professional therapist (whether using music or other mediums) must realize that the unique differences in each person are as important or, in some cases, more important than formal diagnoses. Professional music therapists look beyond diagnostic categories in search of "functional skills" and special abilities that an individual may possess. The following questions are directed to students who are considering or who are in training for a career in music therapy:

1. Is music really *important* to you as a person?
2. Do you have a genuine concern for persons in distress?
3. Are you proceeding under the assumption that music has "magical" powers, or do you understand that, like other health care professions, it is based upon knowledge and research?

Concerning the first question, the authors both emphasize the important part that music plays in their lives. Both agree that without music, they would feel less human, and that it would be difficult to think of life without music. Not everyone may feel this way, but a person considering a career in music therapy may want to weigh carefully the importance of music in his/her life, since it is the principal and essential tool of the profession.

The second question may be more difficult, depending upon the experience of the student. Most university degree programs in music therapy factor in the possible problem some students may have in accepting and adapting to the differences in people who may be assigned to them for purposes of training. From experience, the authors realize that even professionals in clinical settings may not be comfortable working with all types of persons assigned to them. Some who work comfortably with individuals with physical disabilities and/or mental retardation may find it difficult to relate to adolescents needing psychiatric or drug rehabilitation care. If, during the undergraduate years, a student develops a preference or affinity for working with a particular population, it is usually possible for him/her to choose an internship that specializes in that specific population or one very similar.

Question number three is very valid, especially in this age when students are sometimes bombarded by various media with success stories and anecdotes about music as therapy. What some may label "magical" is more than likely only "mysterious," or in other words, those things about the power of music that we do not yet understand. It is because of this need to know more about our medium of choice that we stress the importance of a *scientific approach*, that is, basing our practice upon knowledge and research to provide a rational theory for what we do. Research may also in time find explanations for some of these same mysteries we have recognized but never understood.

Still in the "mysterious" category, since it has not been verified by research, is Gaston's proposal that the aesthetic enjoyment of music reported by many is in fact a necessary part of the human experience found in most cultures and societies—sometimes also described as "spiritual" (Gaston, 1968).

Fortunately, much has been done in the area of research in music therapy that gives strong support to current methods of treatment and great hope for those being developed. Chesky, Michel, and Hummel (1996), after doing research on the use of music and music vibration for pain relief, applied the principles in work with children suffering from post-surgical pain resulting from corrective surgery for scoliosis. Another example is the work of Hurt, McIntosh, and Thaut (1998) in their research on the use of music as a cue to improve walking skills of persons recovering from strokes. In another study, Pribram (1984) determined that extreme repetitiveness of a stimulus (like music) can promote internal inhibition and drowsiness, and too much novelty (which would seem the opposite) had the same effect. This neurological research points to the dulling effect of sensory deprivation or monotony. This information may be significant for the music therapist who is focusing on relaxation techniques.

Another music therapy philosopher-theorist, Sears (1968), along with colleagues in the field, organized the potential therapeutic effects of music into three major areas which he called "Processes." These are as follows:

1. Music provides structured stimuli, which can be organized for therapeutic effects.
2. Music provides opportunities for relating to others.
3. Music provides opportunities for individuals to relate to self.

These processes seem to explain potentials for music therapy in (1) assisting individuals to learn essential information, (2) assisting individuals to learn ways of relating to others in social settings, and (3) assisting individuals to learn to understand themselves and to improve self-esteem.

HISTORICAL PERSPECTIVES

Music Therapy as an "Activity" Therapy

Music therapy traces its recent development to the period following World War II (1945). It is one of a group of *activity* or *adjunctive* therapies that developed during this time, when men and women returning from the war encountered problems with readjustment, post-traumatic stress syndrome, or conditions that were latent before their military experience. Included in this group are occupational therapy (which has the oldest history), physical therapy (which in some form existed prior to this time), recreational therapy, corrective therapy, manual arts therapy, and bibliotherapy (the latter three having been developed mostly in veterans' hospitals). Some forms of occupational therapy, recreational therapy, and even music therapy existed in a few hospitals in the 1920s. At that time, these were usually considered humane ways of providing more constructive use of leisure time.

When music therapy began to be recognized as a part of the therapeutic team, *psychotherapy* was considered by most medical authorities to be the exclusive domain of the psychiatrist. Even clinical psychology was considered as "supportive" in its role of diagnostic testing. Social work was supportive in the sense of providing useful case history material to the psychiatrist and in dealing with troublesome family members. It was generally held that psychotherapy was the principal mode of treatment, and the others were considered to be "supportive."

The **team concept** in therapy began to grow, with cooperation sought between various persons who had significant contact with the patient. Its growth was stimulated by the necessities and realities of the institution and also by a concept known as **milieu therapy**, which was an attempt to control the environment of the patient to promote positive changes in behavior. This was done by carefully describing attitudes and other procedures, which were administered *consistently* by all therapists on the team. One result of this was the idea that activity therapies should be individually "prescribed" by the team "leader," who was usually the psychiatrist (Menninger Foundation, 1945). Today, all of these therapies are recognized as having a more substantial role in treatment.

The Evolution of a Profession

Some writers have referred to music therapy as having "roots" in ancient history, including references to the Biblical story of David treating King Saul with harp music and song for his depression (Michel, 1985). Without further exploration of these historical forebears, we will move on to more recent developments in the field.

The National Association for Music Therapy (NAMT) was founded in 1950, but prior to that time, there had been music called "therapy" in practice at many places throughout the United States just before, during, and after World War II (1941–1945). Historians find instances of music therapy in this country during the nineteenth century and even further back in history in other parts of the world.

Programs like the one established at the Winter Veterans Administration Hospital in Topeka, Kansas, were typical of those evolving from military hospitals after the war. Other programs using music as a kind of therapy (but not always called "music therapy") had been in operation in facilities serving children with disabilities and in state hospitals for persons with mental illness prior to the war (Michel, 1950, 1959, 1985).

The establishment of NAMT brought all of these groups together into a national organization for the purpose of defining and promoting the profession. In 1960, the President of NAMT, in an allegory, characterized music therapy as a "patient" who had been treated for ten years by the association as "therapist" and who had made significant progress toward becoming a new profession in the health services field (Michel, 1960). A second organization, the American Association for Music Therapy (AAMT) was established in 1970. In 1998, it merged with NAMT to form the American Music Therapy Association (AMTA).

A professional credential has been established for music therapists. The designation "Music Therapist–Board Certified" (MT-BC) is awarded by an independent organization, the Certification Board for Music Therapists (CBMT), following completion of a college degree in music therapy and/or other eligibility requirements and passing the national examination.

Those who become MT-BC are recognized by health services providers along with other certified professionals such as Occupational Therapists Registered (OTR) and/or licensed (OTRL), Registered or Licensed Physical Therapists (RPT) or (LPT), Certified Therapeutic Recreation Specialists (CTRS), and Speech-Language Pathologists (SLP). In clinical settings music therapy is sometimes grouped with other creative arts therapies, which include art, drama, dance, and poetry. These are also sometimes called "expressive" therapies.

In clinics where the team approach is used, music therapy is frequently included in decision-making concerning the patients, i.e., diagnosis, and the prescription of a particular therapeutic approach (Michel, 1965). Four factors have contributed to this more significant recognition of the music therapy profession: (1) development of a significant research base and literature, (2) recognition and wider acceptance of learning theory as part of psychotherapy, (3) recognition of the importance of interpersonal relationship—or rapport—that is developed between therapist and patient, and (4) the increasing demands for health services.

American Music Therapy Association

Began in 1950 as the National Association for Music Therapy* →	American Association for Music Therapy founded in 1970 →	Certification Board for Music Therapists (1984) →	NAMT & AAMT merge in 1998 to form AMTA

EMPLOYMENT OPPORTUNITIES

Surveys of the American Music Therapy Association have identified several key areas in which professional music therapists are employed (AMTA, 2003). Many persons work in more than one of these areas. In some instances, the work performed is by contract, and the music therapist is not an actual employee of the provider. The areas listed are geriatric facilities, private practice (self-employed), mental health settings, medical settings, and all others.

Music Therapy in Geriatric Facilities

Music Therapy

A music therapist works in residential or day treatment facilities and provides strategies that encourage independence, orientation to time and place, social interaction, expression of emotions, coping skills, and a healthy self-image. In some instances the music therapist may also serve as the activity director, if he/she has training and interest in that area.

Rationale

Research has shown that music therapy may be successful in helping individuals improve gross and fine motor functioning, improve short-term memory, explore the present moment, express feelings, learn basic music skills or reconnect with those already acquired, and reduce dependence upon medication.

---

* For more information about AMTA go to: www.musictherapy.org

Music Therapy in Private Practice (Self-Employed)

This is a very broad category that includes all services offered by professional music therapists. Below are a few of the possibilities:

Music Therapy Assisting Mental Development

A music therapist assesses each child to determine whether music is motivating and useful in changing behavior. The music therapist may function independently or may be part of an interdisciplinary team. Services may be provided to individual students and/or students in small groups. The therapist may also provide consultation with classroom teachers about effective ways to use music in daily learning activities. The goals of music therapy in this instance could include learning non-music skills; acquiring music skills that may directly affect academic performance; adapted learning for persons with a wide range of problems including developmental delay, learning disabilities, emotional disturbance, severe behavior disorders, and even chemical dependency.

Music Therapy Assisting Physical Development

A music therapist provides services to children and/or adults who have physical disabilities with a usual focus on helping these persons achieve maximum independence and adjustment to their situation. Music therapy may provide a success-oriented environment that enhances self-awareness and self-esteem, and that provides motivation for developing life skills. Goals of music therapy in this instance could include integrating physical, cognitive, and social-emotional skills, increasing motor functioning, addressing problems of heightened or diminished muscle stimulation, minimizing distractibility, and maximizing the use of affected body parts.

Music Therapy and Hospice Care

A music therapist provides services which complement the work of hospice aimed at helping individuals recognize dying as a normal process, addressing emotional and spiritual needs, providing comfort and relaxation, and enhancing personal growth during the process. Goals of music therapy could include increasing the ability to relax and sleep, reducing anxiety and dependence on medication, improving communication (verbal and non-verbal) with significant others, and maintaining or improving the quality of life as long as it shall last.

Music Therapy in Mental Health Settings

The music therapist can design strategies that use the motivating power of the medium to encourage listening, performing, and composing in a way that addresses individual needs. He/she can use music therapy protocols to improve verbalization, explore and confront feelings regarding problems at hand, encourage individuals to begin to take responsibility for their own behavior, and provide experiences that are positive and success-oriented. Services may be provided individually or in small groups (relating to self and relating to others).

Rationale

Research has shown that music therapy may be successful as a means to improve communication skills, minimize negative or inappropriate social interactions, help the individual identify and/or express emotions, improve self-confidence, reduce preoccupation with chemicals, focus on the present, develop new patterns of thinking, recognize hidden abilities, acquire healthy associations with music, develop personal relaxation techniques and other coping skills, and increase positive interactions with peers.

Music Therapy in Medical Settings

Music Therapy

A music therapist works in a general hospital to assist medical doctors and other specialists in promoting a climate with less stress and fostering attitudes that promote healing. The services of a music therapist are especially important in hospitals serving children, who usually have some difficulty adjusting to the clinical environment. The goals of music therapy in this particular instance would include helping children become acclimated to the hospital surroundings and to accept and cooperate with the work of physicians and other professionals as a part of the healing process.

Music Therapy Assisting Surgeons

A music therapist works with the surgeon and the patient to create a healthy emotional climate during stages of pre-operation and post-operation. The goals of music therapy in this instance would include providing music for relaxation and for distraction during procedures required before and after surgery.

Music Therapy Assisted Childbirth

A music therapist works with an expectant mother (and coach) to select preferred music for practicing relaxation, physical and breathing exercises, and for celebration at the actual time of birth. The goals of music therapy in this instance would include increasing ability to isolate and relax muscle groups, discovering source(s) of anxiety and facilitating expression of same, increasing ability to focus attention during the time of contractions, and increasing the mother's feeling of being well-prepared for the birth experience.

Music Therapy in All Other Areas

This was actually the largest category identified by AMTA, probably because our medium crosses many boundaries and provides treatment for the total individual (all skill areas). Other areas could include music therapy used in the treatment of persons dealing with physical or sexual abuse, criminal behavior, cancer, chronic pain, eating disorders, traumatic brain injury, speech impairment, visual impairment, and hearing impairment.

STUDY QUESTIONS FOR CHAPTER 1

1. Briefly describe the difference between **therapeutic music** and **music therapy**.
2. Discuss the idea of music as a **metaphor** for life experiences.
3. What sort of change is implied in the word "therapy"? Is the definition of therapy similar to the definition of learning?
4. State one of the definitions of music therapy given in Chapter 1. In your own words, state your own definition of music therapy.
5. In the early clinical uses of music therapy it was considered an activity or adjunctive therapy. Name at least three other therapies that fall under this category.
6. With the advent of the team concept in therapy, many hospitals adopted **milieu therapy**, which means consistency in the environment of a patient to promote positive changes in behavior. Briefly describe how this was accomplished.
7. When was the organization formerly known as the National Association for Music Therapy and known today as the American Music Therapy Association founded?

8. What do the initials CBMT stand for? What is the purpose of this organization?
9. The text states four factors that have contributed to greater recognition of the music therapy profession. Name them.
10. In comparing Michel's **Music Therapist's Creed** with Pinson's **Music Therapy Philosophy**, what are the four general areas of agreement?
11. Why should a person considering a career in music therapy weigh carefully the importance of music in his/her life?
12. What provisions are in place in the educational process to give a person considering a career in the field more information about various special populations?
13. Is music therapy just a "trial and error" and "mystic healing" kind of thing, or is there clinical research and established guidelines for practice?
14. Name three work settings where music therapists may be employed.

Chapter 2

PROFESSIONAL GUIDELINES

- Principles and Practice
- The Stress Model
- Developmental Skills
- Diagnostic Categories

PRINCIPLES AND PRACTICE

This text will explore both *principles* and *practice* in the field of music therapy. The profession has principles and theories that have been developed through research. The findings of controlled studies take on new dimensions when they become a part of the daily practice of music therapists.

Principle Number One–The ISO Principle

The first general principle of music therapy is the **ISO Principle**. The term "ISO," which means "equal" (from the Greek word *isos*) is used to designate the principle of matching music with an equal behavior or mood of an individual. If music is to be used to reach and change a person, it should begin with matching the medium to the individual's current condition. "Iso-moodic" is a term originated by the psychiatrist, Ira Altshuler (1948).

It is the idea of matching treatment with the present state of the subject, e.g., mood, based upon an assessment of his/her level of functioning. It is the same principle widely used in education, in which the teacher begins instruction at the present level of the student. In the field of medicine it means matching up medications and procedures according to the diagnosis and assessed needs of the patient.

In practice: The skilled music therapist is able to match the style of music to the present needs of the subject and is also able to adjust meter, tempo, volume, and duration to achieve the maximum effect of the **ISO Principle**. The actual use of music in a particular therapeutic situation depends upon the particular needs of the individual, such as:

1. a need for HABILITATION to develop skills that are needed but not already present.
2. a need for REHABILITATION to reestablish lost skills or to replace old skills with new ones.
3. a need for THERAPY to change behaviors on a more immediate basis to provide relief for troubling conditions.

Clinical example: John is a seven-year-old whose hyperactivity and short attention span are creating problems in his public school classroom. It is apparent to all who work with him that he can exhibit better control when properly motivated. During the music therapy assessment, he moves from one instrument to another without spending much time with any of them. He returns to the piano several times, where he plays random keys in a rather erratic way. When the therapist begins to imitate his rhythms in another octave of the piano, John enjoys a moment of "connection" and decides to spend more time with this activity. The music therapist has made the first successful visit to the world of this child by means of the *ISO-Principle*.

Principle Number Two–Protocol Planning

It is important for the professional music therapist to develop **protocol planning**, which may be accomplished by the assessment of every music therapy candidate for indicators of stress and distress and to determine his/her developmental level regardless of age. Assessment will be discussed in more detail in Chapter 3. The therapist may use measurement scales or it may be done through basic behavioral observation and analysis. Such assessment usually follows a review of the patient's medical history and/or a medical examination, which is recommended for all persons receiving treatment. Identification of needs will allow the therapist to prioritize them, directing the area of treatment at those skills most needed by the individual at this point in time. Assessment often also identifies strengths in individual skill areas that may prove useful in the treatment process.

In practice: The assessment process, properly done, will indicate areas of greatest need in each individual. By determining which skills require the most immediate therapeutic intervention, the music therapist can devise a plan that will establish a **protocol** for treatment.

From the very first meeting, this complex interaction is a continuous, concentric circle in which the therapist evaluates and reassesses the needs of the individual served and should be aware of his/her own needs in the therapeutic environment. Through this process, the therapist creates an environment in which the client's needs and responses always receive top priority. The diagram in Figure 3 shows this circle. The process begins at the top with "needs of client" and "needs of therapist."

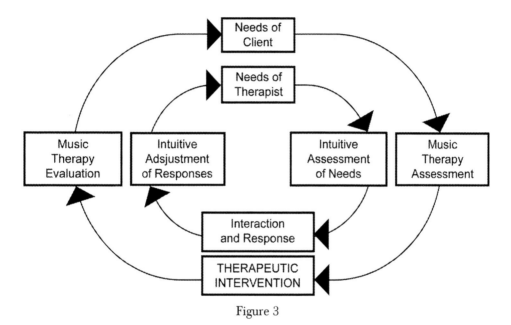

Figure 3

Therapeutic intervention involves the skillful use of the medium of music, which can be likened to a **two-edged sword** (Michel, 1985). One edge is the basic power of music as a sound stimulus (to arouse, to relax, to focus, to enjoy, etc.) and the other the uses to which each society has put music (social dance, symbolic song, performance, creativity, etc.).

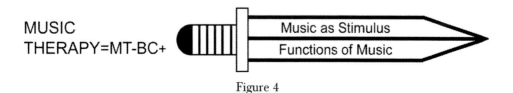

Figure 4

Clinical example: Mary is a six-year-old diagnosed with cerebral palsy. Her speech is very limited, but she is developing some control in the use of her arms and hands. Occupational therapy has recommended that she use a motorized wheelchair as soon as she acquires the skills necessary to operate it safely. Communication therapy is already using a board, which allows her to express her basic needs by pointing. During the music therapy assessment, it is noted that she seems to enjoy playing the large suspended cymbal. Because ***improving her motor skills*** is a prerequisite to controlling a wheelchair and to improved communication skills, the music therapist gives this skill priority and establishes a protocol for treatment. A strategy involving the suspended cymbal is based upon the ***two-edged sword*** (stimulus and function) and will assist the therapist while improving Mary's chances of success in treatment.

Principle Number Three–The Many Faces of Change

During the life span of each individual there is a **constant process of leaving behind or giving up old behaviors and skills**, as new ones develop or are forced upon the person by the circumstances of life. With each change the individual must often go through a natural process of loss or gain, followed by a process of readapting to the new situations (Michel, 1985).

In practice: Music therapy may be used to assist with this process at all levels of development and in the following situations (Michel, 1985):

1. from the comforts of the womb to the realities of the world
2. from normal development to a state of disability
3. from the dependency of childhood to self-reliance
4. from disability to a new life through rehabilitation
5. from disability to an improved quality of life (adaptation of skills)
6. from a comfortable lifestyle to one of pain and/or trauma (either physical or psychological)

The professional music therapist will incorporate processes to assist each individual with the resolution of problems related to change while assisting with the development of compensating skills or new ones.

Clinical example: Marvin is a forty-year-old functioning in the mild range of mental retardation. Following his mother's death ten years ago, he lived with his father. His father was a musician, and through the years provided him many opportunities to express himself through playing the guitar and drums. Last year his father also died, and since that time, he has been living with his older sister. She is not a musician and has had difficulty fulfilling the role that his father played. At the first meeting with the music therapist,

Marvin realized that he had found someone who understood his need to make music, and one who could provide an environment where that need might be fulfilled. In this encounter, the therapist is assisting Marvin in dealing with grief over the loss of his father and also helping him develop his leisure time skills to fill the void that was created. Even though Marvin is an adult, his dependence upon his father was much like that of a child. At the time of this writing, he is entering a phase of his life where he begins to become more self-reliant as a person and learns to use music more independently as a means of self-expression and relating to others.

THE STRESS MODEL

The **Stress and Developmental Skills Model of Music Therapy** (Michel, 1985) appears in Figure 5. It diagrams the effects of stress as it may become distress, which may lead to disease, disorder, and/or disability.

A physician, Hans Selye (1956), pioneered the viewpoint that stress plays an important part in wellness and illness. Without **eustress** (exercising muscles, dealing with life situations, etc.), we would not develop our physical and mental capacities. Everyone experiences a certain amount of **stress**, which may result in mild anxiety, sleeplessness, or other symptoms that are part of daily living. When stress gets out of control or becomes unmanageable, it becomes **distress**. It is at this point that it may affect the immune system and possibly allow the invasion of a **disease** caused by bacteria or viruses. Distress may affect our thinking and possibly lead to a physiological and/or behavioral **disorder**. Some of these conditions could even become a **disability**–rendering the individual incapable of functioning in society without assistance.

There are many diseases, disorders, and/or disabilities that may appear to be unrelated to stress; however, the fields of medicine and therapy continue to discover causal effects. It should be noted that in the **Stress and Developmental Skills Model**, some of the arrows indicating the effects of stress move *from* the condition back to stress levels, because conditions of disease, disorder, and/or disability usually create problems that increase levels of stress.

DEVELOPMENTAL SKILLS

Every individual encounters stressful situations. The types of stress are in many cases related to chronological age and the developmental

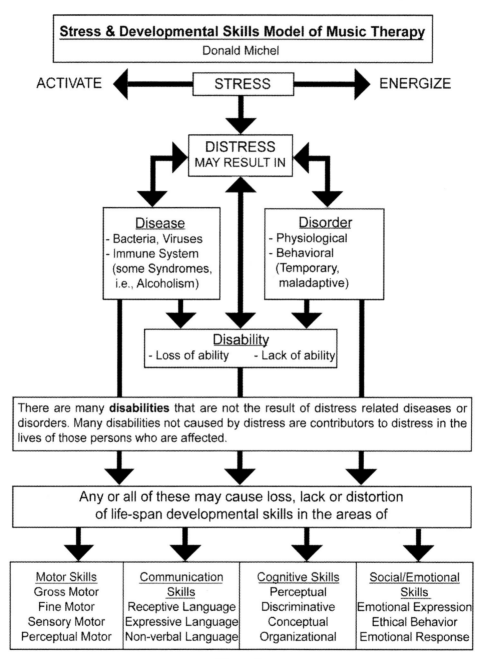

Figure 5

level that one has reached. This concept may be stated as **"different stresses for different stages"** (and individualized therapy might be called "different strokes for different folks").

Developmental levels as based upon the work of Piaget (Flavell, 1971), provide information about the skills that an individual has acquired and which may be compared with those achieved by "normal" persons under average circumstances. Although it is important to know how a person's ability compares with the norm, the immediate goal of treatment would most likely be to help each person progress to a higher level of functioning.

Michel's **Stress and Developmental Skills Model** concludes with the skill areas, which are observable in every individual. It is important that the music therapist have these skills in mind as he/she provides assessment and treatment. Lathom (1981) used an acronym for remembering skill areas. The stated areas are slightly different from those on Michel's **Model**, but this acronym may be a good way to remember this information.

The CAMEOS of Music Therapy

C *communication* skills (same as Michel)
A *academic* skills (see "cognitive" in Michel's model)
M *motor* skills (same as Michel)
E *emotional* skills (Michel combines with social skills)
O *organizational* skills (see "cognitive" in Michel's model)
S *social* skills (Michel combines with emotional skills)

The CAMEOS concept has been expanded to define some of the "skills" which are important to the "development" of music therapists. Just as the therapist is continually evaluating the responses of the individual being served, he/she should also be taking note of the skills that he/she should employ in the therapeutic process (Pinson, 1998).

CAMEOS of the Music Therapist

C *competent* (in music skills, verbal skills, writing skills, organizational skills)
A *alert* (to all of the conditions which are candidates for intervention)
M *methodical* (following a PLAN, subject to necessary adjustments)
E *eclectic* (making use of the best ideas that will benefit clientele)
O *outrageous* (willing to do the "unusual" to accomplish the goals of treatment)
S *sincere* (showing concern for person in treatment and sharing information in a way that is productive)

DIAGNOSTIC CATEGORIES

It is not unusual for a textbook about music therapy to list some of the types of diagnoses that professionals encounter in the field. A list of these under four general categories follows; they will be discussed in greater detail in a later chapter.

1. **Developmental disabilities** include, but are not limited to, conditions such as autism, mental retardation, learning disability, cerebral palsy, and epilepsy.
2. **Psychiatric disorders** include, but are not limited to, conditions such as schizophrenia, bipolar disorder, depression, and social maladjustment.
3. **Physical disabilities** include, but are not limited to, conditions such as paraplegia, quadriplegia, paralysis, impairment of gross and/or fine motor skills, and inability to ambulate.
4. **Behavior disorders** include, but are not limited to, conditions such as hyperactivity, attention deficit disorder, withdrawal, juvenile delinquency, and truancy.

Our preferred usage of these diagnoses, when necessary, suggests putting the word "person" in front of the disability; therefore, one may speak of a person with mental retardation, a person with schizophrenia, or a person with attention deficit disorder. In practice, it is best to refer to an individual by diagnosis *only* when necessary. Overuse or misuse creates the possibility of **labeling**, which leads to less individualized treatment, less respect for each person in treatment, less respect for the family involved, and an attitude that tends to make the label a self-fulfilling prophecy.

In the field of music therapy, it is important to remember that a diagnosis does *not* necessarily imply a specific prescription or treatment. If you have a kidney infection, your doctor usually knows exactly what antibiotic to prescribe for treatment. If you are diagnosed with early infantile autism, there is no one treatment that may be prescribed. It is a mistake to allow a **diagnosis** to be substituted for recognition of a **person** with a disability, disease, or disorder (Michel, 1985).

Persons are often distressed by more than one handicapping condition and are sometimes labeled "multi-handicapped" (Michel, 1985). This term is a very inadequate description. How do you describe a child with poor eyesight, with limited use of his/her limbs, and with intelligence well below the norm for his/her age? Is he or she a person with visual impairment, a person with a physical disability, or a person with mental retardation? Confronting this sort of dilemma, one may quickly see that the term "multi-handicapped" may be inadequate in many instances.

No one is ever handicapped or disabled in only *one* way. There are always social and emotional components. This is sometimes called the ***concept* of multiple handicaps**, i.e., any handicapping event affects more than one part of a person's functioning. It is seldom that one is "just crippled" from say, a broken limb. In fact, the whole social pattern of the individual is changed. Everyone knows that it takes the "will to re-cover" from any kind of disturbance–broken bones, surgery, a crippling disease, or even the common cold. For some of these, it takes longer to recover, and for some persons, recovery is more difficult. In nearly all cases, long or short term, music *can* play a part in the recovery–both in specific applications to basic problems and as an agent to influence the "will to recover," that is, motivation or "morale" (Michel, 1985).

The term "rehabilitation" (like the term "disability") usually implies a much longer, continuing process than "therapy," but the two words are often used interchangeably or in combination. Some professionals are called "rehabilitation therapists." Rehabilitation and/or therapy may focus upon primary and/or associated conditions–in the physical, social, and behavioral (emotional) realms of the individual.

Diagnosis alone does not and should not determine the "placement" of an individual. Many persons with mental retardation, mental illness, and/or a physical disease, disorder, or disability live at home, and many live independently, sometimes surviving in low paying jobs or catego-rized as "homeless." Many persons with physical handicaps and near normal intelligence reside in institutions for persons with mental retar-dation, because other facilities are not equipped to deal with the limita-tions of their physical needs. Many placements are not the result of diagnosis; instead, they result from one or a combination of the follow-ing factors:

1. special needs of the individual
2. family situations (inability to care for the individual at home)
3. lack of facilities in a particular geographical area
4. socioeconomic factors.

It is important to remember that the **Stress and Developmental Skills Model of Music Therapy** is based upon the idea that we should concentrate on the symptoms or results of diseases, disorders, or dis-abilities, i.e., the loss or modification of skills and resulting distress and possible grief. These symptoms provide guidelines for direction of the work of music therapy. This, to us, is far more important than the usual approach, which would be to just use the **diagnosis** rather than a definition of the skill area(s) which need attention. The medical diagnosis and its meaning are very important in understanding the possible limitations associated with a disease, disorder, or disability; however, it is the symptoms and suffering of the individual that should receive priority. In the next chapter, we will discuss ways of further identifying these problems through a basic observation process as the first step in assessment and evaluation.

STUDY QUESTIONS FOR CHAPTER 2

1. Briefly describe the technique known as the **ISO Principle**.
2. Briefly describe the use of the **ISO Principle** in the clinical example (John) that is presented in the text.
3. What sort of information is contained in a music therapy assessment? How does this information help in establishing a **protocol** for treatment?
4. The text mentions the "two-edged sword" which is available to the music therapist. What are the two edges? Describe each briefly.
5. Describe how the skills and needs of Mary were used to establish **protocol** in her music therapy treatment.
6. In discussing **Principle Number Three**, the text mentions six life changes in which music therapy may be of assistance. Name four.
7. Other than the death of his father, what other change(s) or (losses) was Marvin facing?
8. Stress may get out of control to the point that it becomes _____. From that point it may lead to _____, _____, or even _____.
9. Are all disabilities caused by stress? If not, why not? What disabling conditions come to mind that are probably not caused by stress.
10. What are the four skill areas described in Michel's **Model**?
11. Is stress related to chronological age and/or developmental level?
12. Name the skill areas as listed in the **CAMEOS** of Music Therapy.
13. Name the skill areas for *music therapists* in Pinson's **CAMEOS**.
14. How do medical diagnoses sometimes become **labels**?
15. When a diagnosis refers to an individual, how should it be stated?

16. Why is a diagnosis under one of the categories of developmental disabilities, psychiatric disorders, physical disabilities, and behavior disorders not like the diagnosis of an **infectious disease**?
17. Does a particular diagnosis usually determine individual "placement"? Name the four factors that may influence placement.
18. Explain the term "multi-handicapped." Does it adequately describe an individual with more than one disabling condition?
19. Discuss the *concept* **of multiple handicaps** as it is explained in the text.

Chapter 3

MUSIC THERAPY ASSESSMENT

- Observation and Documentation
- Qualitative and Quantitative
- Strengths and Weaknesses

Assessment involves the basic skills of observation and documentation, which are essential tools of the professional music therapist. Everything that we do with the individual in treatment and every behavior that we observe from the very first meeting is part of the assessment process.

OBSERVATION AND DOCUMENTATION

Your interest in music therapy may have developed partially because you are a good observer of other people. The importance of this skill cannot be overly emphasized. It is critical that the music therapist knows about each individual assigned to him/her, and most of this information will be acquired through observation and documentation. If the music therapist is part of a treatment team whose members document what they see and hear (write or record in some manner, i.e., "charting," narrating, or videotaping), this information may be very helpful in learning about each individual served.

What Things Do We Look For?

Certain things that you observe about an individual are difficult if not impossible to measure, but all are important to learning about the skills that will become the focus of treatment. We can use adjectives to describe these behaviors, but they will probably not lend themselves to numerical measures. Below is a list of a few of many of these observable behaviors that are not as easily quantified but still very important to the total picture. These are general observations often made during an initial meeting and are grouped according to the four areas from the **Stress and Developmental Skills Model for Music Therapy**.

> **Motor Skills:** *Activity Level*–Was the individual sedentary, deliberate, hyperactive, fidgety, or lethargic?
> **Cognitive Skills:** *Interest Level*–Was the individual confused, disinterested, curious, cautious, or inattentive?
> **Communication Skills:** *Receptive/Expressive*–Did the individual seem to understand directions, and was he/she able to communicate needs in some manner?
> **Social/Emotional Skills:** *Mood*–Was the individual happy, distracted, confrontational, depressed, quiet, boisterous, energetic, distant, or enthusiastic? *Interaction*–Was the individual friendly, cooperative, aloof, hostile, agitated, withdrawn, gregarious, or careful?

Some of the behaviors above probably fall under more than one skill category, and others *defy categorization*. A person's **appearance** could be described as "well-groomed, unkempt, inappropriate, disheveled, or unusual," but what skill(s) are we describing? Is he/she *physically* unable to do what is needed for good grooming, lacking the *cognitive* ability to make good choices in clothes, wanting to *communicate* something (make a statement), or just trying to be *sociable* and look like everyone else? If someone else is responsible for dressing and grooming the person, *whose* skills are we evaluating?

It is important for the music therapist to make personal note of his/her subjective impression of the person being assessed, i.e., general positive and negative feelings regarding the individual. This information, which usually not a part of the written assessment, may provide a perspective that is important to the treatment process. If the subject of the assessment wishes to express an opinion regarding his/her needs, this should be encouraged and recorded in the assessment.

Following is a list of other behaviors that may be described with adjectives, but these also lend themselves to numerical measures.

> **Motor Skills:** *Fine*–How long did it take the individual to put the pieces in the wooden "shapes" puzzle? *Gross*–How many times did the individual hit the cymbal without interruption?

Communication Skills: *Receptive*–How many times did the individual interrupt the therapist?–a possible indication of a deficit in listening skills. *Expressive*–How many of the five vowel sounds in the song about the states did the individual phonate correctly?

Cognitive Skills: *Perceptual*–How many of the six colors in the song about birds did the individual name correctly? *Conceptual*–How many of the ten locations of objects in the song about "Where do you find me?" could the individual name correctly?

Social/Emotional Skills: *Interaction*–How many of the others in the group can the individual greet by name? *Participation*–In how many of the group activities presented did the individual take part?

How Do We Take Specific Measurements?

The field of behavior modification has developed some measurement techniques that are very useful in recording various things that music therapists observe. Consistent use of these techniques produces data that clearly quantifies progress or lack of same in a particular skill area.

DURATION RECORDING: This is the **length of time** that a particular behavior continues. It could be the number of seconds that an individual plays an instrument, balances on one foot, or sits in a chair. This could be *cumulative* (the total number of seconds during the session engaged in this behavior) or *incident specific* (the number of seconds per incident during the session).

FREQUENCY RECORDING: This is the **number of times** that a particular behavior occurs during a session. It could be the number of correct responses during a music therapy strategy, the number of times an individual left his/her chair without direction, or the number of times that he/she makes eye contact.

The therapist decides which behaviors are *timed* (duration recording) and which are *counted* (frequency recording). In most instances you would *not* employ both for the same behavior.

INTERVAL RECORDING: This technique, sometimes called "time sampling," means that the behavior measured has occurred during a brief interval of time. Hanser (1999) suggests that one of these conditions should be applied:

1. *Individual must respond during the entire ten-second interval.* With this condition and a five-minute space between intervals,we might be able to see that an individual was on task for ten seconds during three of six intervals in a thirty-minute session.
2. *Individual must respond at some time during the ten-second interval.* With this condition and a five-minute space between intervals, we might be able to see that an individual was on task at some time during five of six intervals in a thirty-minute session.
3. *Individual must be responding at the moment of completion of the ten-second interval.* With this condition and a five-minute space between intervals, we might be able to see that an individual was on task at the conclusion of four of six intervals in a thirty-minute session.

With some modification, condition number three is the one that may be the most useful to the music therapist, especially if he/she works alone. The space between the time samples may correspond to the end of a song or other musical conclusion; therefore, the therapist would make note of the behavior being measured at that particular moment of completion. In this way, the sample is measured without any distraction to the strategy.

When the technique of **interval recording** is applied to a music therapy group, the therapist would make note of the number of participants engaged in a particular behavior (attending, playing, singing, etc.) at the end of each predetermined space. This is sometimes called a **planned activity check**. The therapist should also be aware that each individual reacts to musical stimuli in one or more of three different levels of functioning. Observing at which level or levels the individual is most likely responding gives the therapist important clues as to where the person is functioning and where treatment may begin. In terms of **communication skills**, these levels of reaction are as follows:

1. **Receptive**–Individual hears musical stimulus, turns head in the direction of source, and/or smiles. His/her reaction probably indicates that the information has been received.
2. **Perceptive**–Individual hears musical stimulus and identifies it by name, mood, style, tempo, or dynamic. This indicates that he/she has gone beyond reception to *perception.*
3. **Conceptual**–Individual hears musical stimulus "How are you today?" and responds with "fine" or "I'm not feeling well." The response indicates that the listener has probably gone beyond reception and perception to create or *conceive* an answer to the musical question.

Assuming that the individual has good hearing, *Level One* (receptive) response may mean that he/she enjoys the music, or it may mean that he/she is smiling at the therapist for no particular reason. At this level, it may take some very careful observation to determine just what the response means. A *lack* of response at *Level Two* (perceptive) may mean that the individual is incapable of responding at this level, or it may mean that the musical stimulus is one that is not familiar to the individual. It could also mean that at that particular moment the individual simply chose not to respond. *Level Three* (conceptual) response is much more involved than the first two levels. The individual must be capable of processing one and two before adding the extra dimension required in number three. This higher level of response can open doors to many productive experiences in music therapy.

What Is Documentation?

Documentation usually takes the form of a written report of everything that is observed or measured. Many therapists also videotape their sessions to provide a record for review. A written report may be in the form of a narrative describing details of the session, or it may be a checklist of the strategies that indicates level of response. The type of report will most likely be determined by the person(s) and/or the organization(s) requesting the information. Content should be *limited* to the details that are important to assessment and future treatment. One doesn't need to record what the individual was wearing, unless that information is useful to the purpose at hand. If the therapist works with a treatment team, the session report is usually filed in the chart of the individual served. In that way, it is made available for other members of the team to read.

QUALITATIVE AND QUANTITATIVE

Assessment includes all types of observation, including tests, checklists, and any methods used to determine the present level of functioning. This information may be gathered in an initial meeting, but the process is sometimes extended to more than one meeting. The types of assessments used by professional music therapists are sometimes described as **qualitative** and/or **quantitative**. These terms are also used in describing different types of research. The data gathered for an assessment would most likely be a combination of the two.

Qualitative–refers to an approach that uses observation and inter-action, and one which usually does not employ measuring responses or standardized tests

Quantitative–refers to an approach that is based upon measuring responses, either with behavioral observation and/or the use of an informal or standardized test

Qualitative example: Cynthia, age 11, diagnosed with attention deficit dis-order, was referred to the music therapist by her public school for an as-sessment. Since she was coming from another city, the assessment would take place during one meeting with the music therapist. In the waiting room, she seemed anxious about the new environment. Once she entered the therapy room, she went to the piano and began playing individual notes in the center of the instrument in generally organized patterns. The thera-pist joined her and played some moving bass tones underneath her pat-terns. She smiled and continued playing. When the therapist stopped the bass tones, she took his hand and placed it back on the keyboard–a cue to continue the activity.

When offered various rhythm instruments, she explored each one care-fully, trying different methods of producing sound. When the therapist played the guitar, she joined him by strumming regular and sometimes very inventive rhythm patterns. During one of these explorations she initiated speech and said "dig-a-dig-a-doo." Since the meeting was in December, the therapist improvised a song. "Dashing through the snow, dig-a-dig-a-doo, in a one horse open sleigh, dig-a-dig-a-doo," etc. She joined in the response at the end of each line.

She returned to the piano between rhythm activities, and on one of these returns the therapist took her hands and withheld contact with the instru-ment until she said "play" as requested. She was reluctant to offer this verbal response, but she eventually complied with the request, saying some-thing that resembled the word "play." At that point, she was reinforced with more time at the piano.

It was obvious to the therapist that this was a very musical child. She would probably do well in music-based learning activities, and music ther-apy should be helpful in improving her communication skills (speech and following directions).

The information gained about Cynthia in the informal qualitative as-sessment was useful in alerting the public school to her latent musical abilities and to suggest ways of motivating her to better learning expe-riences. Her assessment was a very easy one, since, as stated, she was a very musical child. This process becomes more difficult, when the re-sponses of the individual being assessed are not as enthusiastic or as musically conclusive. The qualitative information, which was video-taped, was later analyzed and converted to quantitative data (Pinson & Michel, 1999, see also Michel and Rohrbacher, 1982). Unfortunately, we were not able to follow the progress of this child in the school setting after the initial assessment.

> *Quantitative example:* Cindy, age 12, with a diagnosis of hypoxic en-cephalopathy was referred to the music therapy clinic. Her disability was a result of respiratory arrest and obstruction of her airway during surgery. Her verbal receptive language was generally good, but her expressive speech was difficult to understand. Her reading skills were very limited, and her writing skills practically nonexistent, because all digits on both hands except the thumbs and forefingers were paralyzed.
>
> An evaluation from communication therapy indicated that her verbal ex-pressive language had shown regression due to decreased control of oral musculature. Improvement had been shown in auditory processing, memory, and printed vocabulary. The music therapy assessment deter-mined that priority needs were improvement in the area of motor coordi-nation and reading skills.
>
> Motor coordination was assessed with a set of twelve exercises based upon four beats. In each of the exercises three of the beats would be played on a drum, and one beat would represent a rest. The rest was alternated to different locations in the beat sequence. Each set of twelve rhythmic sets was played with the right hand and then with the left hand. In the initial assessment she was able to play six sets correctly with the right hand and six with the left hand. At the end of five weeks she was able to play eight sets correctly with each hand.
>
> To get a measurement of her ability to recognize printed material for reading, twenty-five five or six letter words were printed on twenty-five flash cards in large print (because of some visual impairment). During the first session she was able to recognize five of the twenty-five words. This became the baseline for an objective that required her to read these words at each session. Words not recognized were reinforced with a brief song. At the end of five weeks she could recognize ten words.

The general principle of having medical records available to the music therapist before assessment is important if not essential. All therapists must work with the most knowledge possible relevant to the individual who may be a candidate for treatment. It should be noted that the cir-cumstances of referral may sometimes require more immediate attention before receiving the total medical background information that is desir-able. In such cases, music therapy, like all other therapies, must be alert to possible underlying medical conditions that may not have been identified.

In some instances, a music therapist might begin preliminary activities as a step toward a more complete assessment. This might take the form of observing the individual as he/she listens to music—an activity that would require very little physical participation on the part of the patient. Data gained in this manner could possibly be useful to the examining physician, if it contained information that was not observed elsewhere.

Music therapists may use a variety of assessment procedures and forms. It is important to remember that the assessment process is a way of determining the basic needs of each individual of any age and of any diagnosis. These needs will most often be related to skills listed at the conclusion of the **Stress and Developmental Skills Model**. In the assessment process, it is important to look for *strengths* as well as *weaknesses*, since the former is often the key to making improvement in the latter. For instance, a child who has difficulty with expressive language may have good rhythmic skills with his/her hands. The rhythmic skills may be very useful tools in helping this person improve expressive language (pairing rhythms with speech).

Many times, persons are referred to music therapy because someone has noticed certain musical traits. Maybe the individual sings to the radio, or perhaps he/she taps rhythms on the table. If these abilities appear to be better developed than many other skills that the individual demonstrates, they are sometimes called **splinter skills**. Such special abilities may also be found in areas such as memory, mathematics, visual art, mechanics, dance, and drama. It is not unusual to find an individual with significant impairments to general development who has perfect pitch (the ability to recall pitch without reference to a tuned instrument) or near perfect rhythm (the ability to imitate complex rhythms after the first hearing). When these persons are able to demonstrate and possibly develop their special talents in a way that is recognized by society, they are sometimes called **savants**.

STRENGTHS AND WEAKNESSES

Individual strengths are sometimes difficult to determine. If the weaknesses observed seem to be overwhelming, then the therapist may need to look more carefully. If the music therapist should assess a child with no speech, questionable receptive language, the inability to ambulate, and very limited use of hands and arms, it is easy to see that finding strengths may be a very difficult task. Faced with such an assignment the music therapist should look for some of the responses listed below:

Motor Skills: *Fine Motor*–Is there an interest in holding and/or manipulating musical instruments? *Gross Motor*–Is there interest in touching and/or exploring musical instruments?

Communication Skills: *Receptive*–Is there significant eye contact with the therapist? *Expressive*–Is there a response expressed by playing a musical instrument in some manner?

Cognitive Skills: *Perceptual*–Is there a change of facial expression when music is played? *Conceptual*–Is there appropriate laughter when something funny occurs?

Social/Emotional Skills: *Interaction*–Is there an attempt to initiate appropriate physical contact? *Participation*–Is there a a willingness to cooperate?

How is information organized and reported in the assessment process? Methods vary among therapists, and no one in particular is head and shoulders above the others. Following is a copy of the assessment for Cynthia, whose session summary appears on page 35. Since the session summary was very brief, you will note some things in this report that were not apparent in the summary. This format is used by a university music therapy clinic. The name used in the report is fictitious. Note, however, that this name appears *frequently* throughout the report. This repetition is intentional and intended to remind everyone who reads this report of the "person" who is the subject of the assessment.

Music Therapy Assessment

Client: Cynthia　　　　Therapist: J. W. P.　　　　Date: XX/XX/92

Relevant Historical Information

Cynthia is eleven years old and diagnosed with attention deficit hyperactive disorder. She presently lives at home and receives special education services from the XXXXXXXX School District. The school reports that her measurable IQ is 20 and that she does not stay with any one mode of learning long enough to make progress. Teachers have noted on occasion that she taps rhythms or moves her body when music is played.

Profile of Current Performance Levels (Music Skills)

A. *Listening*–Cynthia listened very carefully to the therapist and to music presented during the assessment session.

B. *Moving*–Cynthia imitated movements correctly most of the time, but movements seemed rigid and lacking in control.

C. *Playing*–Cynthia strummed guitar held by the therapist. She also played maracas, suspended cymbal, tambourine, and paddle drum–usually in tempo with the music.

D. *Singing*–Cynthia gave some responses in rhythmic speech ("dig-a-dig-a-doo"), but her ability to match pitch was not measurable during this assessment.

Profile of Extra-Musical Categories (Highest Levels Achieved)

A. *Motor*–Cynthia ambulated without assistance and demonstrated good fine motor skills when exploring the piano and various rhythm instruments.

B. *Cognition*–Cynthia was able to repeat the words "ears, eyes, nose, mouth." She said "ball," when it was given to her during one of the strategies.

C. *Communication*–Cynthia imitated a few words and seemed to understand most directions given to her.

D. *Social/Emotional*–Cynthia assisted in putting instruments away when requested. She smiled and laughed many times during the session. She occasionally resisted following instructions and at times responded with a spitting behavior (not directed toward the therapist).

Area Strengths: Cynthia is obviously a very musical child who enjoyed all activities presented to her. She has developing speech that is understandable. She has rhythmic speech that she can organize into the context of a song. She explores all objects and instruments carefully. She has generally good receptive language, which allowed her to follow most one step directions given by the therapist. Most of her social skills were appropriate.

Area Weaknesses: Cynthia has limited verbal skills at present. She moves impulsively from one activity to another. She has very limited cognitive skills that are measurable. She seldom makes eye contact, and her ability to attend to persons outside her personal space seems limited.

Recommendations (Goals and Objectives)

It is recommended that Cynthia would benefit from music therapy services to improve communication skills and attention to task. These skills should help her make progress in developing cognitive abilities. The following goals and objectives are recommended:

Goal–Cynthia will make progress in the area of communication skills.

Related objective–When given the opportunity, Cynthia will sing 26 of 26 letter names in the song about the alphabet one time per session for three consecutive sessions by December 1, 20XX.
Related objective–While playing a drum with both hands, Cynthia will verbalize numbers in each phrase of "One, Two, Buckle My Shoe" one time per session for three consecutive sessions by December 1, 20XX.

Goal–Cynthia will make progress in the area of attention to task.

Related objective–When offered time to play the piano as a reward for completion, Cynthia will complete a numbers puzzle in three minutes during each session for three consecutive sessions by December 1, 20XX.
Related objective–Following numbered visual cues on a display board, Cynthia will play each of four hand-held instruments in sequence without interruption one time per session for three consecutive sessions by December 1, 20XX.

Services should be provided by a Music Therapist–Board Certified as a direct agent to Cynthia or as a supervising consultant to teachers. Please contact me, if you need the names of qualified persons in your area.

If this clinic provides services, we will continually evaluate and reassess Cynthia's responses and will inform you if and when a point is reached that our services are considered ineffective or no longer necessary.

_____(signature)_____

J.W.P., MT- BC

Note that the *larger portion* of the assessment speaks to the *abilities* of the child, especially in the area of music. It gives a picture of this person that many of the special educators may have never seen before. It gives her parents hope and a reason to be very proud of their child. Do you think these changes in attitude would benefit the child? You can be assured that they would, if the recommendations are implemented. A well-written assessment is the *first* major step toward helping an individual receive music therapy services that may be crucial to his/her development and progress in the educational setting or in any setting where music therapists work.

A professional music therapist providing services for Cynthia might want to utilize the information gained from the **Music Therapy Assessment Profile (MTAP)** that was employed after the initial assessment. This document provided data in developmental terms, i.e., her functional age in most areas, which was determined to be at the two and one half year level. The MTAP indicated some strong areas of functioning, such as her demonstration of music and social/emotional skills. This information could be helpful in protocol planning, which will be the subject of the next chapter.

STUDY QUESTIONS FOR CHAPTER 3

1. The text lists six specific behaviors, which are difficult to quantify. Name three of these.
2. The text lists eight additional behaviors, which would lend themselves to numerical measurement. Name four of these.
3. Describe one use of **duration recording**.
4. Describe one use of **frequency recording**.
5. Would a music therapist normally use duration recording and frequency recording to measure the same behavior?
6. What type of **interval recording** would probably be most useful to the music therapist, especially if he/she worked alone.
7. Discuss the terms **reception**, **perception**, and **conception** as they relate to responses to music stimuli.
8. What techniques are used in an assessment that is called **qualitative**?
9. What things about the client called Cynthia caused the therapist to conclude that she was a very musical child?
10. What techniques are used in an assessment that is called **quantitative**? What specific information was gained from the assessment of the young woman named Cindy?
11. Cindy's progress in motor coordination and reading would most likely be measured with (1) duration recording, (2) frequency

recording, (3) interval recording.

12. Why is it important to assess **strengths** as well as **weaknesses**?
13. Describe what is meant by the term **splinter skills**?
14. What is the term used to describe a person who in the eyes of society has significantly developed his/her splinter skills?
15. One particular word was repeated on purpose several times during the assessment for Cynthia. What was the word?
16. Why is a well-written assessment considered the *first* major step toward the provision of music therapy services for an individual in need?

Chapter 4

PROTOCOL PLANNING

- Post Your Goal
- Setting the Stage for Intervention
- Writing the Objective
- Implementation and Evaluation

T he process of protocol planning involves setting realistic goals (broad, general statements of direction) and related objectives, which contain more specific information about the behavior(s) addressed and estimates of time required for completion. Both goals and objectives are derived from the music therapy assessment. When possible, the needs and desires of the individual in treatment become part of the planning process.

POST YOUR GOAL

When services begin, the music therapist must establish a **goal**, which is simply a **direction** for treatment, as determined by measurable objectives. Think of a **goalpost**, which stands not too far away and reminds the players on a football team which *direction* they need to move the ball. The real "goal" in football is *winning*, and in life, it is *progressing* to a higher level of functioning; however, teams don't always win, and individuals don't always progress to a higher level. Part of football and part of life is learning to handle defeat–either a temporary setback or a permanent loss.

Some therapists talk about long-term goals–things like complete recovery from a disabling condition, leaving an institution to live independently, or becoming a "complete" person. These are all very worthy and in many cases attainable, but they don't offer much in the way of helping us decide which *direction* we should go at the moment.

The goals discussed in this chapter are of a shorter term and will lend direction to our efforts. When a football team makes a touchdown, they *make progress* toward a long-term goal (winning the game), but with each score, they achieve the short-term goal, and this takes them closer to being ahead when the clock runs out. The phrase *will progress* is central in our statement of a goal, which has only three elements:

1. name of the individual (or group) served
2. the phrase "will make progress"
3. name of the skill area which is in need of improvement

Some goal statements may include completion dates (two years, three years, five years). Most of these do not take into account unpredictable environmental and/or developmental changes. We feel that the addition of a "guessing game timeframe" adds very little to the goal-setting process.

Just as a football team has no way of knowing how much time it will take to make the next touchdown, we, as therapists, do not know how long it will take to accomplish the goal which we establish. Therefore, the goal statements recommended here have no timeframe, no measurement criteria, and are all quite simple, as shown in these examples:

John *will make progress* in the area of communication skills.

The members of the music therapy group *will make progress* in the area of social skills.

Jane *will make progress* in the area of fine motor skills.

The skill areas mentioned come from the assessment process, where we determine the areas of greatest need and where we develop protocols for treatment. This information provides the direction for our intervention.

SETTING THE STAGE FOR INTERVENTION

The idea of **protocol**, which was mentioned in Chapter 2, becomes very important at this stage of planning for effective therapeutic intervention. In the example below, George is "selectively" non-verbal and, because of this, an important goal is to make progress in the area of communication skills. The therapist knows that this area of functioning must eventually be addressed; however, this young man has been observed to engage in behavioral outbursts such as tantrums or aggression. These behaviors must be considered and dealt with prior to the implementation of objectives related to communication skills.

To address these disruptive behaviors the therapist should complete a **functional analysis** of the behavior(s) in question. There are three steps in this procedure:

1. Determine what event often *precedes* the onset of the problem behavior. This is called the **antecedent.**
2. Determine what event usually *immediately follows* the problem behavior. This is called the **consequence.** Is this event potentially reinforcing or punishing? What may seem like punishment may actually be very reinforcing.
3. Determine *frequency* or *duration* of the problem behavior.

Clinical example: When George began music therapy, he was ten years old, functioning in the moderate range of mental retardation, and selectively non-verbal (could speak but chose to remain silent most of the time). He would usually respond with the day of the week and the words "music day" during the opening song, and when the "Days of the Week" song was sung, he responded with the first two days but had difficulty with the others. During the music therapy group, he occasionally hit other participants–not the same person every time, but whoever was near to him and "available." Whenever this happened, he was immediately isolated from the group and asked to sit in another part of the room. His attacks did not present any great danger to the others, but they were certainly disruptive to the group and in need of intervention. George seemed to enjoy most of the activities presented by the therapist. Through functional analysis, the therapist determined that each incident of hitting followed George's ceasing to participate in the ongoing activity. Once this information became apparent, the therapist began to watch for the moments when he would stop participating (antecedent). Whenever these occurred, George would be immediately redirected to another activity that was complementary to the one at hand. For instance, if George and the group were playing instruments, and he stopped participating, the therapist would *immediately* hand him a different instrument, compliment him for his participation (change of consequence), and ask him to continue with the new instrument. In most instances, this could be done without interrupting the group strategy. When this plan was put into effect, the incidents of his hitting others were greatly reduced. Before this new plan was put into effect,

George was saying (non-verbally with his stopping), "I want attention." When there was no response, he would engage in hitting to get the attention that he desired.

For many problem behaviors, the solution is not as simple as the example above, but a recommended first step toward solving any problem of this sort is a **functional analysis** to determine just what is happening.

WRITING THE OBJECTIVE

Referring again to the football analogy, the *goal* is making a touchdown. Although occasionally a team makes a great play from their own territory that takes them across the goal line, their immediate **objective** is to move the ball forward ten yards for a first down. Continuing to achieve this objective, they will eventually reach the goal line (if the clock doesn't run out).

An **objective** is an *immediate focus* of treatment, which includes a specific, measurable outcome, a condition for achievement, and a projected time of completion. The objective for the football team is to move the ball at least ten yards in four or less downs. More specifically, a music therapy objective contains the following items (not necessarily stated in this order):

1. name of person or group receiving treatment
2. observable behavior that will be performed or eliminated
3. measurable criteria for completion
4. estimated time required to complete the objective
5. condition for completion (with prompts, unassisted, during a particular song, while standing, while seated, etc.)

WARNING! The word **behavior** in the objective statement refers to *anything* that an individual does or does not do. It does not necessarily mean a "behavior" in the sense of that which is inappropriate; however, it may have that meaning in an objective.

Before an objective can be written, the therapist must determine the criteria that will be used to measure completion. To know where an individual needs to go, we must first find out where he/she is at the present time. This process is actually an extension of the **ISO Principle**, in which the therapist adjusts his/her strategies to the present functioning of the individual. For the football team, it is enough to know that they are on their own twenty-yard line, and that their objective is to reach the thirty-yard line within four downs. The music therapist needs specific information related to the behavior that will be addressed. This is called a **baseline**. A **baseline** is a measurement of present functioning relative to a particular behavior before therapeutic intervention. Ideally it should be determined through a series of observations displayed on a graph. If the therapist had created a baseline for "George," the graph would have shown that during one session, he hit others three times, in the next, he hit twice, and in the third, he hit four times.

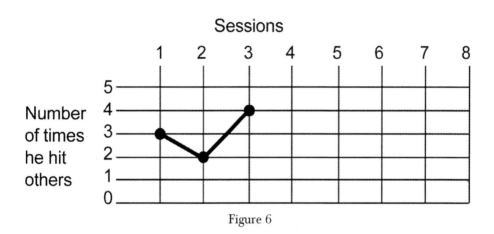

Figure 6

Since this was described as a "pre-objective" stage, the therapist may not have written a formal objective; however, if one had been written for this behavior, it would probably have been worded in this way:

When redirected by the therapist (condition) **George** (name) **will reduce incidents of hitting others** (behavior) **to zero per session** (criteria) **by the end of the month** (time).

Because we need concrete data to show progress, no progress, or regression, it is desirable to write a music therapy objective to provide a framework through which this may be accomplished. Many factors have to be considered, in order that the specific behavior is addressed and that the focus of treatment represents the most pressing needs of the individual receiving services (**protocol**).

Below is an easy way to remember the "ingredients" of a good objective. It is a "piggy-back" song (new words to a familiar tune).

Writing An Objective (Pinson)

(to the tune of *If I Were A Rich Man*)

Writing an objective, do-re-mi-fa-so-la,
yah-da, yah-da, yab-ba-dab-ba-doo.
If you are a therapist of note, this is what you ought to do.

Every objective—must say **who*** and **what***
and **when*** and **where*** and—**how much.***
With these basic elements in place,
therapist and client keep in touch.

You could impress us with your keen understanding
of the diagnosis and its cause;
and quote all of your sources without pause.
You could write long and glowing phrases
that tell us who you are and what you do.
And we know that every word is true; but,

Writing an objective, do-re-mi-fa-so-la,
yah-da, yah-da, yab-ba-dab-ba-doo.
It's a simple exercise that you
must learn how to think and how to do.

***who**—name of person receiving treatment ***what**—observable behavior person will perform ***when**—estimated time of completion ***where**—the condition under which this will happen ***how much**—measurable criteria for completion.

A respected colleague, Kathleen Coleman (1998), has suggested the idea of writing **SMART Objectives**. The following questions about the behavior or skill should be addressed as we determine the focus for treatment:

S – Is the behavior described *specific* to the needs of the individual?
M – Is the behavior *measurable* in concrete terms?
A – Is the behavior really *attainable* by this individual?
R – Is the behavior *realistic* in the music therapy setting?
T – Is the behavior attainable in the *time* available for treatment?

To this list, another may be added to create a more complete evaluation of the objective (Pinson, 1999). By asking the questions below, we can be more certain that the objective has real **VALUE** for the individual.

V – Does the objective have real *value* for future development?
A – Does the objective *agree* with those suggested by others?
L – Does the objective *lead* to attainment of greater skills?
U – Does the objective specify skills that are *uppermost* on the list of needs for this individual?
E – Does this objective target a need that may be addressed *effectively* by music therapy?

Considering the example of George, the therapist might now be ready to write an objective that would help him move forward and make progress in the area of communication skills, which had been identified as needed. The therapist knew that George rarely answered a direct question, except the one before the opening song, "What day is it?" In order to encourage him to answer more direct questions, the therapist might explore the possibility of his requesting an instrument to play during the rhythm activity. If he responded with one single word request during the first three sessions, the therapist could write the following objective:

Using a five word sentence (condition), **George** (name) **will request an instrument** (behavior) **one time per session for three consecutive sessions** (criteria) **by the end of the semester** (time).

Nothing about *methodology* appears in the statement of the objective. This information would be included in a **music therapy plan**. Such a plan would include specific step-by-step instructions for implementation. This information could be available for review by a supervisor and/or for use by another person in the therapist's absence. It might also provide a more definite statement of the specific behavior (sometimes called a **target behavior**), which is the projected outcome of the objective. In reality, this **plan** is a way of developing *protocol* within the music therapy session.

The plan does not need to state the obvious, i.e., "therapist enters room." The plan does not need to address issues such as placement of instruments, position of the therapist and client during the session, or other basic considerations—*unless* these are considered critical to the outcome of therapy. With regard to the objective that might be written for George, the complete *plan* would include the following steps:

1. Before the rhythm activity therapist holds up an instrument (for instance, a tambourine).
2. Therapist says, "If you want to play the tambourine, please raise your hand."

3. If one or more than one person indicates an interest, the therapist asks one person, "_(name)_, what do you say?"
4. If the person knows and is able to respond appropriately, he/she will say, "May I play the tambourine?" Therapist hands the instrument to the person, instructing him/her to place it on the floor until everyone has made a selection.
5. If the person does not respond or gives an incomplete response, the therapist will say, "let's all *sing* it," leading the group in singing "May I play the tambourine, the tambourine, the tambourine? May I play the tambourine? May I play it, please?" (tune: *Merrily We Roll Along*)
6. Therapist asks again, "_(name)_, what do you say?" If there is an incomplete response, the therapist accepts this and gives the instrument to the person, telling him/her to put it on the floor until everyone has made a choice.

The detailed instructions, which would be used with all persons in the group that George attends, are really designed with his objective in mind. With careful planning, a competent therapist may implement and measure individual objectives during a music therapy session with a small group of persons (maximum of six recommended).

IMPLEMENTATION AND EVALUATION

There is *no way* to predict the outcome of a well-written objective and a good plan before they are actually placed in operation. It is important to remember that progress toward an objective is *rarely* a series of *upward* moves toward the target behavior; however, out of the "ups and downs," one can usually see a *direction* for the objective. After a baseline has been established and the objective written for George has been implemented, there are several possible outcomes:

1. George has good days and bad days, but, as shown in Figure 7, the general direction is upward toward the target behavior.

Figure 7 illustrates a fairly *normal* line of progression for a person with special needs. If these were weekly sessions, the therapist might be well past the projected date of completion (depending upon the date of implementation); however, since George has demonstrated progress toward the objective, it will probably be kept in place until completion.

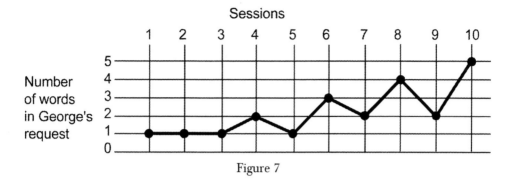

Figure 7

2. After establishment of baseline (session #3), George responds with a five-word request for the next four sessions.

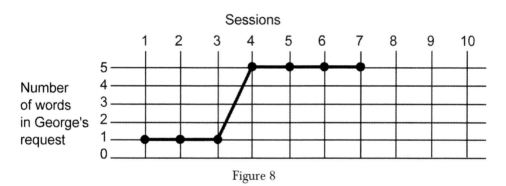

Figure 8

A situation like that shown in Figure 8 is rare, but a music therapist must be ready to accept and applaud a victory such as this and to write a brand new objective based upon current information. This indicates that during the initial assessment process the therapist may have received some responses that did not represent the maximum ability of the individual. In the case of a person who is selectively non-verbal, such a change could occur very quickly, since the basic skills required for speech are already in place.

3. George remains near baseline or below for several weeks. Figure 9 clearly indicates little or no progress.

At the point of completion of ten sessions, the therapist can see that George has made no significant progress beyond the baseline. At this time the therapist would probably consider one of these options:

1. Change the **plan** that is in place for implementation of the objective. Since a good therapist is evaluating during every session, it is

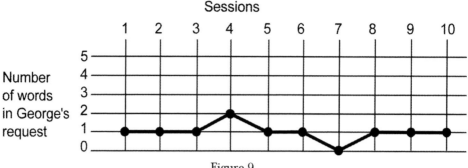

Figure 9

possible that adjustments have already been made with no improvement in response.

2. Change the **task** used in the objective. Perhaps George is not properly challenged with just asking for an instrument. He might respond to a task that required more cognitive ability, even though this skill is not the focus of the objective.

3. Change the **reinforcer**. Perhaps George is not properly motivated by receiving the instrument as reward for a complete request, especially if he knows that he can receive it without a request.

4. Change the **objective** in hopes of finding one, which will produce more positive results in the area of communication skills. If this is done, it may be wise to re-establish a baseline.

Unlike the objective written for George, some objectives established by music therapists are not so easily measured on a continuing (session by session) basis. When the situation demands, music therapists use what is known as **pretest–posttest**. A **pretest** of a particular skill or condition, such as managing one's anxiety, is given before treatment begins. In some situations the test may be given at intervals during treatment, but most of the time, progress is evaluated at the conclusion of the treatment plan. One such test is the Spielberger State-Trait Test of Anxiety (1980). It measures a person's immediate state of anxiety and also one's general condition (trait) of tension. If such a test were used in conjunction with a stated objective, it would be similar to this:

During the music therapy session (condition) **Frances** (name) **will reduce her anxiety level** (behavior) **as shown by the Spielberger State-Trait Test** (criteria) **by the end of the treatment plan** (time).

If a therapist is going to use **pretest–posttest** as a means of measurement, there are two concerns that need to be addressed:

1. Does the test measure what its designer(s) say it will measure? This characteristic is known as **validity**.
2. Does repeated use of the test produce similar results? This characteristic is known as **reliability**.

Most standardized versions of **pretest–posttest** have been developed with these characteristics in mind. With regard to *validity* the developers have often compared scores on the test to measurements of other criteria related to the behavior (or skill). If this additional data supports the conclusion of the test, then it is probably valid. With regard to *reliability*, the developers have used the test with several individuals, conducted interviews to determine how different people interpret the questions, and made modifications to accommodate varying levels of understanding. Another way of measuring *reliability* is to document the *consistency* of a test when it is administered several times to similar individuals or groups.

A standardized **pretest–posttest** may not be found or may not be useful in all situations. Experienced music therapists sometimes use self-made tests for pre/post evaluation. These may be in terms of specific developmental skills such as the ability to greet appropriately, the ability to follow simple directions, and/or the ability to relate to peers in a cooperative way.

Effective **Protocol Planning** includes everything discussed in Chapters 3 and 4. This includes assessment based upon all information that is available to the therapist, planning for intervention (with behavior modification when necessary), establishing goals and objectives, and measuring progress when it occurs.

Providing a place to begin (the **ISO Principle**) through assessment not only makes any therapy more directed toward possible progress or improvement of the individual, but it is also a form of *accountability*, that is, being ethically responsible to the individual being treated. By seeking knowledge about the person's problems and making planned efforts to assist him/her to make improvements, the music therapist is *not* a "problem fixer" but one who can in many instances help others "fix" themselves. A responsible music therapist will *disclose* this information before treatment. This and other considerations of ethical behavior will be discussed in a later chapter.

STUDY QUESTIONS FOR CHAPTER 4

1. In the practice of music therapy, a **goal** is simply a _____ for treatment.
2. The real "goal" in football is **winning**, and in life, it is _____ to a higher level of functioning.
3. If George's primary need is in the area of communication skills, how will we state his **goal**?
4. In the process known as **functional analysis**, the event which usually *precedes* the onset of a problem behavior is called the _____.
5. The event which most often immediately *follows* the problem behavior is known as the _____.
6. In the case of George, what was the problem behavior that had to be brought under control before addressing his communication skills?
7. An **objective** is an _____ _____ of treatment.
8. Name the five key ingredients of a good objective.
9. How do those ingredients interface with the "piggy-back" song about writing an objective?

   Who = _____

   What = _____

   When = _____

   Where = _____

   How much = _____
10. Name the five characteristics of a **SMART** objective.
11. Name the five elements of assessing **VALUE** in an objective.
12. Define **target behavior**.
13. What four *changes* does the therapist consider if it becomes clear that the individual in treatment is not making any significant progress?
14. What is a **pretest–posttest**? When is it likely to be used in therapy?
15. Define **validity** and **reliability** as they relate to pretest–posttest.
16. Are **standardized** tests the *only* ones used for **pretest–posttest**?

Chapter 5

MUSIC THERAPY AND MOTOR SKILLS

- Preliminary Considerations
- Causes and Conditions
- Gross Motor Skills
- Fine Motor Skills
- Very Limited Motor Skills
- Habilitation and Rehabilitation

PRELIMINARY CONSIDERATIONS

This chapter will discuss some of the techniques used by music therapists in the treatment of persons with physical disabilities or in need of help in the habilitation or rehabilitation of motor skills. Most of the techniques described may be useful with persons of all ages; however, we recognize that developmental differences and individual experiences will be factors in each person's capabilities and limitations, and these will be determined by assessment that includes both strengths as well as weaknesses.

Since these factors directly affect and are affected by the levels of stress and distress in each individual, it seems reasonable that we should begin by assessing stress, including both physical and psychological aspects. If stress is determined to be a factor in the functioning of the individual, we might implement a procedure such as relaxation to music to assist the person in treatment to consciously control his/her level of stress. Pain is usually considered distress and may also benefit from relaxation to music.

It should also be pointed out that the basic principles of developmental life changes, as they relate to loss of motor functioning, are factors that may need attention, depending upon the age and life experience of the person in treatment.

CAUSES AND CONDITIONS

Physical disabilities and all motor disorders and diseases resulting in problems of locomotion and coordination arise from a large variety of sources and causes. There may be difficulties during birth itself, prenatal conditions such as disease, or trauma encountered in an accident. The information offered here is very general in nature, and the authors acknowledge the need for professional music therapists in some instances to gain a more complete and comprehensive knowledge of these conditions. For example, poliomyelitis, which became rare in the U.S.A. in the 1960s after the widespread inoculations of the Salk vaccine, is now almost completely eliminated around the world. In addition to "polio" (sometimes called infantile paralysis), other diseases cause physical disabilities, especially those that attack brain or central nervous system tissue, such as encephalitis and meningitis. Since damage to the central nervous system is not easy to correct, and because these tissues in most instances do not regenerate and replace themselves, disabilities are usually permanent.

One condition that causes physical disabilities is cerebral palsy (CP). In a sense, CP is a form of brain damage, since tissue may be destroyed from insufficient oxygen (anoxia) during the birth process. Many persons with cerebral palsy have normal or superior intelligence. In most cases, the parts of the brain that have been damaged seem to be those that affect the control of muscles involved in everyday motor skills. This differentiates these persons from those who have other types of brain injuries and who may suffer greater impairment, including mental, due to damage to other parts of the brain. Other causes of physical disabilities and motor disorders include spinal cord damage, e.g., spina bifida, paraplegia, and quadraplegia. Amputations (sometimes due to a disease such as diabetes), rheumatoid arthritis, muscular dystrophy, and severe burns may also be causative in physical disabilities.

As music therapists begin their training, some will, for the first time, encounter individuals with severe physical disabilities. This may be in a nursing home, in a residential facility for persons with developmental disabilities, or in a rehabilitation unit of a general hospital. A first reaction of some students may be one of mild shock. Others may encounter cases, more traumatic, which might lead them to the conclusion that "this is not an occupation for me." With further experience, most students will find that the persons with such severe disabilities have similar needs, expectations, families, friends, hopes, fears, dreams, and the desire to succeed. When this becomes apparent to the novice, he/she may be able to adapt more quickly. It should be noted that when persons with physical disabilities are seen in a productive musical environment, their common humanity becomes more apparent.

GROSS MOTOR SKILLS

Gross motor skills refers to the ability to control the larger muscles of the body–those that allow the head, trunk, arms, hands, legs, and feet to move in different directions as needed. In many instances individuals are able to *move* the larger body parts but lack the control necessary to make the movement useful.

Adaptations: Physical

During music therapy assessment with persons who have gross motor problems that may or may not be considered disabilities, it may be discovered that some environmental or physical adaptations are necessary for treatment. Reports from occupational and physical therapists may contain information about adaptations that have already been used with an individual. Some of these may be incorporated in treatment by a music therapist when appropriate. The relationship between gross motor skills and musical ability will also, in most cases, be determined during the music therapy assessment.

When the individual receiving treatment can make gross motor movements in the arms or legs, but lacks the ability to grasp an instrument or a mallet, padded strips of velcro may be used to attach an instrument or a mallet to the limb that can be moved.

Occasionally, a person may be able to strike a stationary drum with the hand alone or manipulate a shaker or "ocean drum" using only gross motor skills. Music therapists also have been able to teach persons who have only head movement to play keyboard melodies using a pointer attached to the head. Electronic switches have been developed which require minimal pressure to close. These may be connected to devices that will ring a handbell, strike a drum or tambourine, shake a maraca, and start or stop a tape recorder or CD player when needed by a person with severe motor disabilities.

Adaptations: Selection of Instruments and Music

Persons with severe deficits in gross motor functioning may or may not have good *control* of motion; and therefore, the music therapist should not expect regular patterns of rhythm to be produced in many cases. When we hear a drum or temple blocks, we generally expect the sound to be "beat oriented" (in syncrony with the beat of the music stimulus). A good quality suspended cymbal struck with a soft mallet or brushes creates a sound that is acceptable with or without beat orientation. An "ocean drum" or "rain stick" creates sounds that we actually *expect* to be without beat orientation.

Pentatonic scales (tones 1, 2, 3, 5, & 6 from any major scale, or the black keys on the piano) offer an excellent "field of play" for persons whose coordination skills make playing at an exact moment or in an exact place on an instrument difficult if not impossible. These pentatonic notes may be played randomly by a person with physical limitations to create a satisfactory accompaniment to many melodies that are played or sung.

It may be useful to "answer" whatever sound the person can produce in a way that is meaningful. Experienced music therapists are often able to improvise "around" the sounds created by an individual with limited abilities, and when this is done, these expressions take on new meaning. They may even become a non-verbal dialogue between the individual and the therapist. If a person is able to produce something akin to a regular beat, the therapist's improvisation will be based upon the tempo established by the individual. Both of these adaptations by the therapist illustrate the use of the **ISO Principle**, mentioned earlier.

Accommodations: Alteration of the Therapeutic Environment

Positioning of the individual and/or the instrument is critical to the success of some music therapy strategies. Experimenting may be necessary to find the correct placement and angle for mounting an instrument for the special needs individual. Support for those parts of the body not being used in a particular activity may be necessary in order to promote more independent activity and control of muscles. All possibilities must be explored to achieve good results (Clark & Chadwick, 1979).

Clinical example: Mary was ten years old and diagnosed with cerebral palsy, which was caused by anoxia (oxygen deprivation) during birth. She had limited use of her limbs, was strapped into metal braces on her legs and arms, and confined to a wheelchair most of her waking hours. She could only make a few vocal sounds. She was referred to the university music therapy clinic, because her mother noted her smiling and making simple movements and sounds when music played on the radio.

During the first session, her sparkling eyes and attention to the therapist seemed to indicate that Mary understood much of what was spoken to her. She was receiving services of physical therapy to increase blood circulation and prevent atrophy of the larger muscles and communication therapy to encourage vocalization and the formation of words.

The music therapist began by playing the autoharp and singing familiar folk songs from selections recommended by Mary's mother. Music therapy student assistants attached rhythm instruments to Mary's arms and legs to increase the power of the stimulus. During certain selections, she moved her arms and hands and attempted vocalization. Her movements seemed to be inhibited by her being strapped in her wheelchair. With the mother's permission, the therapist removed Mary from the chair and allowed her to lie on a pad on the floor, where she had more freedom to move both arms and legs in spite of her braces. In response to the question "Do you want to make music?", she would move her legs and smile to indicate her desire to participate.

Further objectives included having Mary raise one leg, over which she had control and strike the floor with her foot as a signal for the music therapist to begin singing or to continue. Eventually the therapist was able to adjust his beat and tempo to the moments when Mary struck the floor, which she did at a regular but slow pace to give signals to the therapist (an example of the **ISO Principle**).

One of the songs that Mary loved was "Home On The Range." An objective was developed in which she filled in the word "home" at the appropriate place in the song.

In the case of Mary, the therapist began with *assessment* as a qualitative observation of her functioning and skills. Reports from physical therapy and communication therapy and information from her mother helped the therapist develop a plan for involving Mary in making music aimed at achieving therapeutic goals. A major *accommodation* (allowing her to lie on the floor without the restrictions of the wheelchair) was a very important part of the therapeutic process. Planned *adaptation* (selection of appropriate music) also proved to be the key to her being able to respond vocally, i.e., with the word "home."

Use of the ISO Principle allowed her to become an integral part of the production of music as a form of communication and physical activity during the sessions, which were part of her medically prescribed needs.

Michel's note: Mary was my *teacher* and had great influence on the music therapy students as well. From our first meeting, I could tell how much this child loved music and how much this experience meant to her. There were no formal assessment tools in music therapy available at that time, so we proceeded with the information given, coupled with careful observations during every session. When circumstances forced the termination of our relationship, I knew that, although Mary still had much to achieve, she had made significant progress during our time together. She taught the students and me many things, and her enthusiasm challenged us to make the most of our—and her—abilities in the therapy setting.

FINE MOTOR SKILLS

The term "fine motor skills" usually refers to the more precise use and control of the hands and fingers. This definition should probably include more precise use and control of the feet and toes, since some persons have developed these skills in an outstanding way. Other fine motor skills involve muscles of the face, tongue, and throat, which are used in communication (speech production) and in basic survival skills (suckling for infants).

Adaptations: Physical

The ability to grasp an object is found in many aspects of musical expression. Any handheld instrument or a mallet or drumstick may be used, but in some cases, adaptations should be considered. Some persons who may be able to grasp a ball with no difficulty experience problems with cylindrical shapes (such as a drumsticks or rhythm sticks). Some manufacturers have offered sticks and mallets with an enlarged surface for ease of holding. An individual may be able to hold instruments of larger diameter (claves) more easily than those of a smaller diameter (Orff instrument mallets). A small stick may be lengthened and enlarged by adding a wooden dowel as shown in Figure 10. Cut dowel to the length needed for grasping. Drill a hole with same diameter as the mallet in one end of the dowel. Insert the mallet in the dowel. Add wood glue if the mallet does not fit snugly. If adding the dowel creates a mallet that is too long, trim the mallet before inserting it in the dowel.

Figure 10

The *texture* of a handheld instrument may make it more difficult to hold. Hard surfaces may be changed to soft by the addition of foam rubber. The cylindrical foam strips (used for pipe insulation and available at home improvement stores) are excellent for this purpose.

Adaptations: Selection of Instruments and Music

Electronic keyboards offer a wide range of possibilities for persons with limited fine motor skills. Using the "chord" mode with "automatic rhythm," a person can play a limitless number of melodies with accompaniment using only a single digit in each hand.

An open-tuned guitar (tuning shown in Figure 11) may create many possibilities for someone who has difficulty fingering chords in the traditional manner. With open tuning, one simply "blocks" across an entire fret to create a new chord. Positions may be color-coded to identify chords. Melodies or simply lyrics with chords (also color-coded) may be used as "lead sheets." Guitars purchased for these purposes should have narrow neck surfaces. For *all* guitars used by individuals in treatment, *nylon* strings are recommended. Metal strings may sound better to some ears, but they are *not* "user-friendly" to inexperienced players.

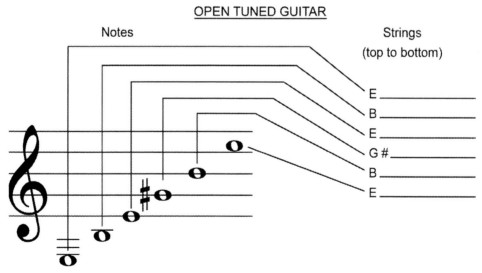

Figure 11

Music for persons in treatment (most of them with little or no music experience) should be chosen with regard to their interests, their chronological age, their mental age, their ability to learn, and, according to the focus of this chapter, their physical abilities. It is not appropriate to offer "children's" music to adults, even though they may be functioning in a lower developmental range. It is a challenge to find "adult" music that is less complex, but it can and should be done. Music such as folk songs, in many cases, defies categorization and may be appropriate for persons of any age.

The ability to find and sometimes rearrange music for use with persons with motor impairment is an important skill that should be acquired by music therapists. In all cases, instruments and music should be chosen with the idea of providing each individual a *successful* experience that will allow him/her to make progress toward the identified goals. Such experiences may also achieve reduction of distress and increase self-esteem in the process.

Accommodations: Environmental Considerations

The *size* of certain surfaces of musical instruments may be a concern for persons with physical disabilities. If a person finds it hard to control the direction and force of a mallet, assigning him/her to a glockenspiel (which has *tiny* metal bars) would be a mistake. A bass xylophone or metallophone (with larger bars) would improve the chances of success for this person. There are also bass tone bars with very large surfaces for striking, which also require less demanding, i.e., less frequent rhythmic responses from the participant. Electronic keyboards with *small* keys that would be frustrating to anyone except a small child, and especially to a person with limited fine motor skills, should be avoided.

Clinical example: Larry was twenty years old and diagnosed with Apert's Syndrome, a rare condition that causes malformation of the head and face and limited development of fingers and toes. His speech consisted of "grunts" to indicate yes and no. He could read simple words and was able to print a few key words to make his needs known. Extensive facial-cranial surgery had given him a slightly more "normal" appearance, but it was still apparent that his development was unusual.

At the first meeting, the music therapist found that Larry had a well-developed sense of humor and a will to survive which was nothing less than outstanding. Adaptations were considered, since Larry's fingers were not fully developed; however, it was found that he could hold a mallet without the use of any special equipment.

On the drum, he demonstrated very good rhythmic skills, and he was also able to repeat short melodic patterns on the metallophone. It was decided that progress in communication skills and leisure time skills were priorities, so objectives were put in place to help him learn to read and write one new word at each session and to learn to play one song on the metallophone by rote each month.

Larry became one of the key figures in the percussion ensemble at the facility where he resided, he made progress in his communication skills, and he was able to win several awards at the annual state music festival for persons with developmental disabilities. He also learned to play single finger melodies accompanied by single finger chords on an electronic organ, and an instrument of this type was eventually made available to him at his residence, in order that he would have an alternative to watching television during leisure time.

In the case of Larry, music therapy began with a qualitative **assessment** of his skills. **Adaptations** were considered, but it was found that he could complete the musical tasks assigned to him without special devices. Percussion **instruments** (metallophone and drum) were chosen, because these were the most accessible to him, and because he seemed to find real joy in playing them. **Music** began with basic intervals, which the therapist would play and Larry would repeat. These grew into full melodies, which he memorized after hearing them a few times. The **accommodation** of having his own electronic keyboard at his residence opened new doors for him to practice new songs at his own pace.

Pinson's note: Larry's appearance was so very "unusual," that I first thought community audiences who came to see the percussion ensemble would find it very difficult to watch him with any degree of compassion and understanding. I was *wrong.* My own immaturity and lack of experience at the time caused me to have these feelings, and in retrospect, I realize that I was probably concerned about my *being seen* in public with this young man. Wherever the ensemble gave performances, Larry's enthusiasm and display of above average music skills always won the audience over. The dramatic change in my own attitude reminded me of the phrase offered to me by the first music therapist I ever met, who frequently pointed out that in this business, the real question is "therapy for *whom?*"

VERY LIMITED MOTOR SKILLS

This poem was written for a music therapy intern after her first encounter with an individual with severe physical disabilities.

There you are,
barely able to move,
unable to speak–
and here I come,
guitar in hand,
to sing a song for you.
I really don't know
whether you enjoy my music.
I see you smile,
but I don't know what it means.
Perhaps you are just amused
at my feeble attempts
to reach out to you.
I know from my own experience
that one can be thinking
some very neat thoughts
without moving a muscle.
I apologize for my frustration
in trying to reach you.
I trust that there
is purpose in your being,
and that if I fail,
you will think of a way
to reach me. (Pinson, 1981)

Many persons working in music therapy encounter individuals whose motor skills are extremely limited. This can be very frustrating, as voiced in the poem at the left. A smile may be a good indication of response, but the skilled therapist will probably look for other responses, especially in the area of motor skills, which will give the therapeutic interaction more meaning and validity. Many persons with very limited motor skills are able to make movements that are at first very difficult to detect–perhaps a slight motion of an arm or leg, the ability to move the head forward or to the left or right, or even the blink of an eye. These are clues to the type of *involvement* that is best. This may take the form of vocalizing (if that is an option), playing an instrument with adaptation, or simply *making choices* regarding the content or type of music that will be used in the process.

HABILITATION AND REHABILITATION

In using music therapy to address a person's progress in the area of motor skills, the therapist needs to have realistic expectations regarding the outcome of treatment. **Habilitation** means developing skills that have never been acquired by the individual. **Rehabilitation** involves helping a person to regain skills that have been lost due to distress, disease, disorder, or disability.

The therapist should understand his/her role as one involved in the habilitative and/or rehabilitative process. Obviously, a very thorough assessment of the individual seeking treatment is necessary. In both habilitation and rehabilitation the music therapist often relies on assessments provided by physicians, occupational therapists, and physical therapists. Much of the information from other sources has not been gathered in a setting that involves music; therefore, it is important for the music therapist to carefully observe the individual's response to musical stimuli.

One such formal assessment is the **Music Therapy Assessment Profile–MTAP** (Michel & Rohrbacher, 1983) developed for assessment of all the major areas of skills of children in their first three years, using procedures assessing the skills in or under music conditions. A few other such assessments using music have been developed, but the music therapist may still be able to observe the skills that have been assessed under more formal procedures by other professionals (OT, PT, etc.) and by observing the person informally while he/she participates in music activities.

In both habilitation and rehabilitation, outcomes of therapy may be measured in terms of skills learned or relearned. The term **habilitation** often applies to younger individuals who have not learned developmental skills appropriate for their chronological ages. When new skills are learned, i.e., in both gross and fine motor areas, it can be equally rewarding for the person and his/her therapist alike. In relearning skills (walking or speaking again), the outcomes may be more comparable to and based upon skills that were originally present. The music therapist should try to determine what musical skills may have been present in the person prior to the need for therapy, in order to be able to utilize whatever residuals that may be present. In many instances, the outcomes of music therapy intervention may exceed those of other conventional therapies due to the attractiveness, motivational aspects, structure, and expressive nature of the medium–music.

The case of Mary, in this chapter, illustrates the power of music to motivate and stimulate–even to structure–motor and speech functioning; however, it also illustrates that a person with her disability has severe limitations, which may be lifelong and most likely intractable. There is hope in the fact that all individuals, with or without disabling conditions, go through similar stages of development which may directly affect their ability to acquire new skills.

With regard to rehabilitation, persons with impaired motor skills due to strokes, automobile accidents, or other injuries that cause brain damage have shown positive response to music therapy. Research in this area, such as that of Staum (1983), which studied gait problems of individuals in a hospital setting and how to use music to regain such skills, is helpful as a reference for music therapy protocol planning. In the 1990s and into the twenty-first century, Thaut and associates (1990, 2000) developed scientifically based methods aimed at assisting stroke victims to regain motor skills, especially in the areas of walking (gait) and balance. The research team included physicians, physical therapists, and other professionals. They developed what is called "Rhythmic Auditory Stimulation" (RAS), which helps cue the stroke victim's brain activity to stimulate improved gait, using music that is carefully chosen and controlled.

How may students of music therapy learn about these new techniques? During undergraduate training, the student learns to read and understand research such as that described above. Graduate students learn the techniques of research to not only become knowledgeable in understanding and using new scientific developments in their academic work but also to be able to apply basic research techniques, i.e., evaluation of results, in their music therapy clinical procedures. Some produce and publish their research to contribute to the body of knowledge that is the foundation of the music therapy profession.

STUDY QUESTIONS FOR CHAPTER 5

1. Most of the techniques described in Chapter 5 are intended for what age group?
2. Name three possible causes of physical disabilities.
3. Does the condition of cerebral palsy always affect the intelligence of the individual?
4. What is the central message of the poem about persons with very limited motor skills?
5. Define gross motor skills. In many instances, individuals are able to move the larger muscles but lack the _____ necessary to make the movement useful.
6. Name three adaptive devices that have been used successfully with persons with impaired gross motor skills.
7. Name three instruments that may be played successfully without reference to a beat.
8. How does a music therapist create a non-verbal instrumental dialogue with an individual with a physical disability?
9. In the case study of Mary, how did the selection of music provide the key to her actually forming a word?
10. Define fine motor skills? Should this definition include the use of feet and toes?
11. Name two instruments recommended for persons with limited fine motor skills.
12. What important lesson did Larry "teach" the music therapist?

13. Habilitation means developing _____ which have never been acquired by the individual in treatment. Define rehabilitation.
14. Does the music therapist need to adjust his/her expectations when working with persons who are severely physically disabled?
15. In the research of Thaut, the initials "RAS" stand for: (a) reading and science, (b) regular attendance schedule (c) rhythmic auditory stimulation.
16. Why is the open-tuned guitar more accessible to persons with physical disabilities?
17. The initials MTAP stand for _____.

Chapter 6

MUSIC THERAPY AND COMMUNICATION SKILLS

- Preliminary Considerations
- Conditions and Causes
- Receptive and Expressive Skills
- Music Therapy Intervention

PRELIMINARY CONSIDERATIONS

Music is often considered a form of communication. It has been said that if words could express all human feelings, music would never have been invented. Music's *primary* role may be that of providing another form of communication–especially in the area of feelings and emotions. Its *secondary* role is that of being a "modifier" of other forms of expression. When words are set to music, the meaning is usually enhanced and clarified, e.g., musicals, operas, movies, etc.

Since music plays a significant role as a primary and secondary means of expression, music therapy is one of the most valuable means of addressing needs in the area of communication skills. Sears (1968) stated that music provides (1) STRUCTURE, i.e., in terms of passage of time but also in the underlying forms of musical expression; (2) a way of RELATING TO SELF; and (3) a way of RELATING TO OTHERS.

When one thinks of communication, the words "speech" and "language" are usually prominent sub-categories. Speech Language Pathologists (SLPs) and Audiologists provide much valuable information in the assessment and treatment of communication problems. In many instances, music therapy develops objectives that will complement the work of these professionals.

Communication means different things to different people, but for the professional educator or music therapist, it always includes the two aspects of SENSORY PERCEPTION and BEHAVIORAL RE-SPONSE, i.e., by voice, writing, and non-verbal means such as facial and bodily expression and/or movement. Although some may occasionally use smell (olfactory) and taste (gustatory) in certain activities, we will leave these for the most part to the domains of aroma therapy and behavior therapy, except for those instances when individuals report such sensory responses while performing and/or listening to music (synesthesia).

The **basic skills** of communication include the following:

Visual Skills
- Reception (the ability to see)
- Perception (including identification and comparison)
- Conception (developing ideas from visual information)

Auditory Skills
- Reception (the ability to hear)
- Perception (including identification and comparison)
- Conception (developing ideas from auditory information)

Tactile (or Tactual) Skills
- Reception (the ability to feel)
- Perception (including identification and gaining meaning from encountering a variety of surfaces, e.g., Braille text for the blind, conditions, temperature, motion, and behaviors such as hand-shakes, hugs, etc.)
- Conception (developing ideas from tactile information)

Speech and **Language Skills** develop from the **basic skills** above.

Understanding the development of communication skills is very important for music therapists and many other professionals as well. How can music facilitate communication? There are many examples of music therapists treating individuals for problems that occur in the areas of hearing, visual, or tactual modalities. Many individuals who seek the services of music therapy are experiencing difficulty in the area of communication. At one extreme, there are those who are able to communicate—but not effectively—and therefore find themselves feeling separated from the rest of the world. Persons with developmental disabilities or those who have suffered traumatic injury may find it difficult to communicate even their basic needs. Still others may have acquired inappropriate or destructive ways of communicating that hinder development in the area of social/emotional skills and learning. Music therapists are often challenged to deal with these problems, sometimes as a basic priority to continuation of therapy in other areas.

Communication **skills** include the areas of **reception, perception,** and **conception.** When we discuss deficits in the ability to communicate, the following problems are specific to the sensory mechanisms involved:

1. **visual impairment**–mild to profound loss of sight
2. **hearing impairment**–mild to profound loss of hearing
3. **speech impairment**–the inability to speak and/or to produce standard speech patterns
4. **tactile impairment**–mild to profound impairment of the sense of touch
5. **language impairment**–mild to profound impairment of the ability to understand and/or reproduce symbols (verbal and/or non-verbal) required for communication

CONDITIONS AND CAUSES

The conditions and causes of **visual impairment** may be categorized in four areas:

1. **protective** (eyelids and tissue surrounding the eye)–includes infections such as "pink eye" and *gonococcal conjunctivitis*
2. **refractive** (iris, cornea, and lens)–includes *anterior uveitis* (inflammation of the iris), *keratitis* (inflammation of the cornea), *cataracts* (lens disorders), *myopia* (severe elongation of the eyeball), and *glaucoma* (abnormal pressure in the aqueous fluid)
3. **directive** (muscles involved in eye movement)–includes *strabismus* (sometimes called "crossed eyes") and *nystagmus* (rapid involuntary movement of the eyeball)
4. **receptive** (retina and optic nerve)–includes *retinitis pigmentosa* (hereditary degeneration and atrophy of the retina), *optic atrophy* (degeneration of nerve fibers connecting the retina to cells of the brain), and *detached retina* (caused by fluid from the overlying choroid tissue)

The conditions and causes of **hearing impairment** may be categorized in three areas:

1. **conductive loss** (from the outer ear to the inner ear)–includes wax buildup in the ear canal, damage to the ear drum, and diseases of the middle ear (infections, excessive pressure)
2. **sensorineural loss** (cochlea, auditory nerve)–includes destruction of the cochlea by disease or excessively high sound levels and damage to or destruction of the auditory nerve
3. **central loss** (central nervous system and brain)–includes stroke, tumors, injuries, and causes difficult to diagnose or describe

It should be noted that *most* problems related to **conductive loss** may be *improved* by medical or surgical treatment. The problems associated with **sensorineural loss** are usually *permanent*; however, research and experiments in medicine and surgery, e.g., cochlear implants, are already showing great promise in this area. Problems related to **central loss**, which in most cases defy diagnosis or description, are at the present time considered not treatable.

According to Michel and Jones (1991) and Miller (1982), the conditions and causes of **speech impairment** may be categorized in four areas:

1. **articulation**–includes *substitutions* ("tan" for "can"), *omissions* ("pay" for "play"), *distortions* ("th" for "s"–sometimes called a "lisp"), *apraxia* (inability to control muscles used in speech, even though they work well in non-speech activities), and *dysarthria* (paralysis or coordination problem in speech musculature)
2. **fluency**–includes *primary stuttering* (repetition of speech without any awareness of abnormality) and *secondary stuttering* (avoiding certain words and situations because of awareness of the problem)
3. **voice**–includes *pitch* (may not be appropriate for the person's age or sex), *intensity* (too loud or too soft in specific situations), and *quality* (rasp, hoarseness, and/or other unpleasant sounds)
4. **delay**–includes *receptive aphasia* (loss of ability to understand speech) and *expressive aphasia* (inability to produce speech).

With regard to aphasia, it should be noted that it may affect only a single aspect of language use, such as the ability to retrieve the names of objects (*receptive*); however, in some instances, multiple aspects of communication may be impaired (*receptive* and *expressive*).

The conditions and causes of **language impairment** fall into three major categories:

1. **delay**–the inability to communicate in the code of the community at a specific developmental age, usually related to short

attention span, poor auditory memory, and/or geographic displacement
2. **receptive**–the inability to understand complex sentences and/or unusual use of words.
3. **expressive**–the inability to produce complex sentences and/or unusual word phrases appropriately

The conditions and causes of **tactile impairment** may be categorized in at least four areas:

1. **loss of proprioception**–difficulty sensing the position of the limbs and their movements
2. **tactile defensiveness**–a dysfunction (possibly learned) in which tactile sensations are amplified to the point that they cause distress
3. **loss of tactile discrimination**–difficulty discriminating between shapes, textures, sizes, etc. through touch
4. **loss of reflex**–a condition (possibly learned) which inhibits withdrawing from pain, reaction (startle) to surprise situations, and various responses to vestibular stimulation

RECEPTIVE AND EXPRESSIVE SKILLS

Speech language pathologists use the terms **receptive language** and **expressive language**. In their discipline, the word **receptive** includes both *perception* and *conception* (terms discussed in Chapter 3). **Receptive** and **expressive** may also be applied to the basic skills of communication. The following chart compares the two terms:

Skill	Receptive Indicator	Expressive Response
Visual	blinks eyes or makes other movement in response to a flashlight	identifies source of light as flashlight
Aural	startles or instantly reacts to the sound of a cymbal	identifies sound as that of a cymbal
Tactual	grasps ball when given the opportunity	identifies object as a ball

At the **receptive** level, it may seem that nothing has been *communicated.* The *message* to the therapist at this level is: (visual)–"I see something." (aural)–"I hear something." (tactual)–"I feel something." These messages, which are in a sense also "expressive," tell the evaluator that the receptive skill is working. Each message has been communicated by the *actions* (basic reflexes or learned behaviors) of the person involved.

Expressive skills usually require more than "reflexes" to identify the stimulus. Identifying the flashlight (F), the cymbal (C), and the ball (B) could be done in many different ways, which may include:

1. individual speaks (F), (C), or (B)
2. individual uses sign language to indicate (F), (C), or (B)
3. individual points to the word (F), (C), or (B)
4. individual points to a picture of (F), (C), or (B)
5. individual writes or types (F), (C), or (B)
6. individual points to letters that spell (F), (C), or (B)
7. individual triggers a communication device which electronically *speaks* (F), (C), and (B)

More specific evaluation of basic communication skills is included in the *Music Therapy Assessment Profile* (Michel & Rhorbacher, 1983). Further information regarding these skills may be found in *Music for Developing Speech and Language Skills in Children* (Michel & Jones, 1991)

MUSIC THERAPY INTERVENTION

It is obvious that there is a strong correlation between communication skills and cognitive skills. The examples given here will *focus* on the basic aspects of communication, but in all situations, the cognitive (as it relates to understanding what is being communicated) will be present and in many cases be an important part of the measurement criteria.

Music Therapy for Persons with Visual Impairment

The techniques described here are those used by music therapists who work with persons with visual impairment. They can generally be used with persons of all ages, but it is obvious that a child in his/her developmental years encounters problems that are totally different from those which might be faced by an adult who loses vision as the result of disease or an accident.

When the music therapist is asked to provide services for a person with visual impairment, the first step would be an assessment to determine the severity of the condition and also provide some indication of how music might play a part in the therapeutic process. In most instances, a person who is referred for music therapy has probably already been evaluated by a physician to determine whether the condition affecting vision is progressive, temporary, permanent, or treatable. This information will be useful in establishing a direction for treatment and developing protocol based upon the developmental model of distress, disease, disorder, and disability.

Visual impairment is, for the most part, related to **receptive** communication. Although we can communicate emotion (and perhaps truthfulness) with our eyes, their more important function is that of being a *major* source of information about the world around us. The music therapist will in many cases be an "interpreter"–who assists the individual in understanding the things he/she cannot see. Music is an effective medium for this task, since it contains ideas organized in a way that stimulates understanding. In this respect it may offer new insight where other approaches fail. The premises below should be understood thoroughly before attempting to assist persons with visual impairment in improving their communication skills.

Limited Concepts

A person who has had very limited vision from birth gets all or most information through the other areas of communication–aural and tactual. This person may have speech that is somewhat fluent, and he/she may be able to converse about a wide range of subjects, but the absence of useful sight from an early age probably means that *real* understanding of everyday language may be seriously deficient. The exceptions would be persons who have received a thorough regimen of instruction from professionals who specialize in this sort of training.

Appear Normal Much of the Time

A person with significant visual impairment may demonstrate the ability to ambulate without assistance, make conversation, recognize others (usually by the sound of their voices or their "scents"), and perform most self-help skills. In reality this individual's knowledge of his/her world is probably very limited and may have large gaps in the storage of information regarding things such as appropriate dress, social cues, different surroundings, safety concerns, and the ability to function independently.

Aural and Tactual Skills

Many persons with visual impairment have greater development in the areas of aural and tactual skills that may make them excellent candidates for music therapy. Music is a world without pictures (except in a theatre context and popular videos) that may be easier for them to understand. It may become a *means* of communication that they have never experienced and a possible key to more stability and purpose in life. Perfect pitch is not unusual among persons with visual impairment. This, plus their ability to imitate sounds, opens doors for accomplishment in the area of vocal music. Many do well in tasks that require finger dexterity (such as the use of Braille or playing the piano). It is also possible that the heightened development may be in only *one* area–aural skills *or* tactile skills. If there is a deficiency in the area of tactile skills, tasks such as writing one's name or buttoning a button might be very difficult, if not impossible. Having information about other skill areas gives the therapist more ideas about possible treatment.

ADAPTATIONS

For the person who has moderate visual impairment and good cognitive ability, the therapist will probably enlarge print for reading skills–including words numbers, and music notation. Lightboards (Pinson, 1999) are excellent as cuing devices for playing hand-held instruments (bells, chimes, etc.). There are also electronic sensors, which may be triggered to touch the skin gently as a cue for performance.

Lyrics of songs may be adapted to coincide with the abilities of the singer. In Willie Nelson's *On The Road Again* (1980) he has a line that says "seeing things that I may never see again." A useful adaptation would be "doing things that I may never do again." Some individuals do not require this sort of adaptation, since they feel that they "see" with their other senses. If a person who has no sight says, "see you later," don't argue. "I see" also means "I understand."

Instrument and Music Selection

The piano and other keyboard instruments are "naturals" for most persons with visual impairment. Their very logical organization of tones makes them very accessible. The electronic keyboards with built-in rhythm sections and automatic chord formation are *not* recommended, since they offer little challenge and opportunity for developing tactual skills. If vocalizing is a mode of treatment, the songs should be *age appropriate* and also experience appropriate. With regard to the latter, the material should describe things that the individual has experienced– or those which he/she would be capable of experiencing if given the opportunity.

ACCOMMODATIONS

For purposes of complementing life skills training, which the individual has probably received or will be receiving at some time, the therapy room should be organized in a way that will encourage as much independent movement and exploration as possible in a "safe" environment. This concept could be extended to having the individual find his/her way from another location to the therapy room. The person in treatment should also be encouraged to locate instruments and/or objects within the room. Music might be the motivating factor that would provide the necessary reinforcement for completion of this very important task.

Clinical example: Angie, age 12, with a diagnosis of autism and severe visual impairment, was referred to the music therapist after her caregivers noticed her singing along with the radio. Her appearance was normal, and her vocabulary sufficient for communicating her needs. She had a marked distrust of new people and new environments–possibly a result of some instances of sexual abuse.

Any changes in her routine were met with throwing herself on the floor and scratching her arms. For this reason, the music therapist came to her residence for their first meeting. The therapist and an intern were greeted with a smile when they were introduced as music therapists. During that first session, Angie sang (always on pitch), played rhythm instruments with advanced patterns, and immediately figured out the chord progressions on the Omnichord for "Five Foot Two" (not your usual "I-IV-V" tune) after hearing the intern play them *one* time.

Sessions continued in her residence for two months. At that point, the therapist asked Angie to walk with him and the intern to the music therapy room (about three blocks away on campus). That first trip, she followed reluctantly with verbal prompts. Once she found that the therapy room contained a lot of instruments (including a *real* piano), she required no more prompts to make the trip.

Up to this point, all sessions had followed a "ritual" format, with each activity in its "predictable" place. After a few sessions in the therapy room, the order of activities was changed (on purpose). The therapist knew what to expect. Angie threw herself on the floor. The behavior was ignored, since she had learned to perform this stunt without injuring herself. She did not scratch her arms–an attention seeking behavior that would have required intervention. During sessions that followed, Angie progressed from playing the Omnichord to forming chords on the piano. After four months, she could play all major and minor chords in "circle" order, and she could also use them to accompany some of the songs that were sung.

Rates of self-injurious behaviors at her residence began to decrease, and although she threw herself down a few more times during music therapy sessions, she eventually learned that this behavior had no effect on the structure determined by the therapist.

Progress in all areas continued, and at age 16, Angie was moved to a group home in the community. Her chord vocabulary had expanded to include major and minor seventh chords, diminished seventh chords, and ninth chords. She learned to play keyboard accompaniments for a local handbell choir composed of persons with special needs, and for three summers, she participated in the annual tour, which was three days and two nights of *multiple* changes of routine in several different locations. For this young woman, music had become her *primary* mode of communication–allowing her to say things that she could never say before and to experience life in a new dimension.

Music Therapy for Persons with Hearing Impairment

Many persons with hearing impairment find music a very satisfying world with which to affiliate. In many instances it is a *non-verbal* world, where there is no need to understand language and no need to perform vocally. As stated previously, the two components of communication skills are **receptive** and **expressive**.

Receptive–We depend upon hearing for much of the information that we receive.
Expressive–We learn to speak by imitating those whom we hear. If we do not hear as we should, speech is slow to develop (if not impossible).

The ability to hear may also have a dramatic effect upon one's ability to *communicate* through the medium of music–especially in the area of receptive language. Even with devices that amplify sound, persons with hearing impairment may not receive stimuli that is as meaningful as that received by persons with normal hearing. It may be also said that in some instances, persons with hearing impairment develop more interest in the vibratory aspects of musical instruments and recorded sound, i.e., feeling the head of a drum or the surface of an electronic speaker.

ADAPTATIONS

If the individual has sight and his/her cognitive level will permit it, the therapist should establish a strong link between visual cues and the production of music. This could be done with charts that indicate the appropriate time to clap hands, engage in certain movement activities, or play a percussion instrument (pitch oriented or non-pitch oriented).

If the cognitive level of the individual does not allow the use of charts, the music therapist may try direct cuing (pointing to the individual at the time a response is desired). Should the person be visually impaired *and* hearing impaired, the therapist should explore tactile cues (playing when touched on the arm by the therapist or by means of an electronic device controlled from a distance).

It is usually difficult to determine whether or not a person with hearing impairment is receiving much auditory stimulation from the music strategy at hand. Many individuals gain a sense of pride and accomplishment–regardless of whether they hear enough to appreciate the auditory aspects of the music making. These persons have in many instances been excluded from other group activities that required hearing, and they are usually very happy to be included in some way.

Instrument and Music Selection

Persons with hearing impairment may enjoy playing any musical instrument; however, large instruments (such as the bass drum and bass tone bars) and instruments with more overtones (such as handbells and cymbals) may offer the best opportunity for some auditory stimulation, which adds quality to the musical experience.

Selection of music would largely be determined by the cognitive ability of the individual, his/her chronological age, and individual preferences. The principal guideline for selecting music used in therapy is: **Less is usually more.** It is more important for a person to have a successful experience with music that is less demanding than to have an unsuccessful or "half-baked" experience with music that is too difficult.

ACCOMMODATIONS

Any hearing devices that may assist persons with impairment should be used. These would include those worn by the individual and amplification of instruments used. Placement near sound sources or near the director for individual cuing would be important. If the person with hearing impairment also has physically disabling conditions, special electronic switches for triggering sound and adapted methods of holding instruments may be appropriate.

If the person in treatment knows some type of sign language, the therapist should acquaint himself/herself with appropriate signs for basic communication that might be needed in the music therapy environment. Words such as *sit, stand, play, rest,* and *watch* me would be a very good place to start. Beyond that the ability to sign the person's name, your own name, the months of the year, and the days of the week would be helpful.

Clinical example: Wanda was fifteen years old and diagnosed with profound hearing impairment when she began receiving the services of a music therapist. She had been placed in a residential facility for persons with mental retardation because, at the time, there were no appropriate schools or programs for the hearing impaired in her area, and because her behavior at home had become unmanageable. She had basic sign language skills and could read some printed words but had never learned to write. Her inappropriate behaviors seemed to be linked to boredom, inactivity, and the feeling of isolation that was created in part by her inability to hear. She could make vocal sounds, but none of these resembled words.

Communication therapy developed a program to improve her sign language skills, she was given training in the sheltered workshop to improve her on-task behavior, and the music therapist developed objectives that complemented those of the other disciplines.

She became a member of the sign choir—a group composed of persons with hearing impairment and some with normal hearing who wanted to learn more about sign language. These persons were taught to sign to the words of songs, which the school choir sang or which were available on recordings. When the sign choir performed with the vocal choir, at least two therapists were required (one to lead and/or accompany the singing and a second to lead the sign choir by modeling the appropriate signs in the proper sequence). A person from the communication therapy department was usually willing to assist as director of the sign choir for these performances. When disciplines can cooperate in this manner, the chances for individual improvement are greatly enhanced.

After a successful experience with the sign choir, Wanda was allowed to join the handbell choir. She learned to follow charts composed of color-coded letters, and her attention to task during this experience was outstanding. In spite of her hearing impairment, she somehow received enough auditory stimulus from the handbells to be able to sense when her neighbors in the choir did not play on time or when one of them would occasionally ring the wrong bell. Her behavior problems in the sign choir and bell choir were minimal, because she was fully involved in these activities.

After moving from the residential facility to a group home in the community, Wanda continued her handbell experience in a local choir made up of persons with developmental disabilities. The move to the community brought with it some new challenges with regard to her behavior. She began to have more contact with persons who *expected* a certain level of compliance, and there were fewer persons available to her who could communicate with the basic sign language that she knew. In spite of these factors, she was regular in her attendance at rehearsals and performances, suggesting that the bell choir was still very important to her as a social outlet in which she felt comfortable and a place where she could receive some recognition for her efforts.

Music Therapy for Persons with Speech Impairment

With problems of speech the music therapist should *always* work in careful consultation with a speech-language pathologist. Many of these professionals are very eager to have other therapies to complement their own, because in many cases the problems encountered are rather severe and difficult to treat.

ADAPTATIONS

Two aspects of speech that are usually addressed by music therapists are pitch and rhythm. It is important to determine the voice range of the individual, in order that exercises offered are in a range that is workable. Development of pitch variation is important to all persons, regardless of whether or not they are capable of singing. The proper use of speech in communication requires pitch variation. With regard to rhythm, the therapist needs to determine whether the person in treatment responds best to creating his/her own rhythm while speaking, or whether the rhythmic stimulus is more effective when produced by the music therapist. Rhythm exercises may be the key to improved pronunciation, because rhythm, like speech, occurs in **real time**, i.e., in the moment, instantaneous.

Instrument and Music Selection

If instruments are used in conjunction with speech development, the type of instruments used would be determined by individual preferences and by the cognitive and motor ability of the person in treatment. Basic rhythm instruments would probably be most useful, since the amount of thought devoted to these would be minimal and allow the person to do speech exercises without confusion of priorities.

Music selection would usually be based upon some individual preferences and by the type of speech problem encountered. Some songs require only a single-syllable response (if that is appropriate). Most require *timed* responses, but in some cases, the sound is more important than the rhythm.

ACCOMMODATIONS

The information received from the speech-language pathologist would be helpful in deciding about the types of accommodations that might be used. A mirror that allows the individual to see his/her sound production during speech may be helpful. A microphone and amplifier (with or without electronic sound modification) is sometimes useful. A tape recorder for playback of speech/music exercises may help promote learning. Persons who have no speech but who communicate with a computerized device that produces speech have been successfully integrated into music ensembles by creative music therapists—much to the delight of the individuals and those who support them.

Clinical example: Karen first received music therapy services when she was eighteen years old. At age fifteen, she had been involved in an automobile accident that left her in a coma for several weeks. During recovery, the first signs of returning speech were words that she would fill in here and there, when her favorite country and western recordings were played. Before the accident, she had sung in a church choir and occasionally done solos.

A report from her communication therapist indicated that she had made good progress in producing vowel sounds, but many of her consonants were still very difficult to understand, especially "k" and "s." She also had trouble sustaining sound long enough to complete a sentence.

At the beginning of treatment, the music therapist determined that Karen's vocal range was only six semitones (from F# below middle C to middle C on the piano). A song was written for her within this range that consisted mainly of dotted half notes moving in 3/4 time. The text of the song was religious in nature, but because of her church choir background, Karen (and her mother) approved its use in her music therapy program. Initially Karen could accurately match about 50 percent of the pitches in the song. Her ability to sustain the dotted half notes was also about 50 percent. Because of her problems in pronouncing some consonants, the song was at first very difficult to understand. Before the conclusion of treatment, she was able to sing the song with 90 percent accuracy on pitches and 90 percent sustaining dotted half notes. Intelligibility on this particular song was nearly 100 percent.

The music therapist encouraged Karen to continue to sing along with her country western recordings. He also prepared a tape of the special song for her to practice at home. The use of a harmonica during sessions and at home proved useful in helping her to breathe more deeply, which allowed her to sustain vocal sounds longer and also gave her more breath to assist in producing consonants such as "b" and "p." The focus with the harmonica was not to produce melodies but sustained chords (a tonic chord when blowing through the instrument and a dominant chord when inhaling air through the instrument). During sessions, the therapist would improvise sounds at the piano that complemented these chord changes.

Treatment at the university music therapy clinic continued for four semesters. Services were terminated because of other priorities in the family schedule, and because they were driving forty miles each way to get to the clinic. Karen's speech and ability to sing had shown significant improvement. Her vocal range was extended three semitones. Her speech was still slow and at times difficult to understand, but with her will to work and an outstanding desire to achieve, the prognosis for continued improvement was very good.

It should be noted that, in spite of terrific family support and a very positive atmosphere, there were a few times when Karen arrived very discouraged and in no mood for serious work on her objectives. The music therapist was sensitive to these situations, and during these sessions, he would get ideas from her for songs, which were improvised on the spot. Karen, who has a great sense of humor, would usually find something to laugh about before the session was completed. Music, when used properly, has the power to change the mood of an individual from "gloom and doom" to "ease on down the road." As music therapists, we must always remember that we not only assist persons in developing or regaining life skills, but our intervention helps them cope with the present situation in which they find themselves.

Music Therapy for Persons with Tactile Impairment

For many persons involved in music therapy, tactile (or tactual) impairment is not the *focus* of the intervention, but difficulties in this area present a special challenge for the therapist. There are at least two types of tactile impairment that may be more important in the development of communication skills:

1. *tactile defensiveness*–characterized by hypersensitivity to touch and usually expressed by withdrawing the part of the body that has come in contact with another person (or a particular surface).

This type of tactile impairment sometimes causes an infant with autism to withdraw from the touch of the birth mother.

2. *loss of tactile discrimination*–characterized by the inability to properly identify or conceptualize surfaces (such as a person with visual impairment finding it difficult to learn Braille).

Either condition may be neurological (related to brain damage or lack of development) or behavioral (possibly a choice that the individual is making to get attention or to avoid involvement).

Either condition would probably get in the way of establishing communication with other persons and/or becoming acclimated to a new environment. The challenge for the music therapist is to find ways in which participation in musical activities may be used to improve these skills beyond their present level or to create a "safe" working relationship that allows development of other communication skills.

ADAPTATIONS

If the individual in treatment withdraws from touch, the music therapist has options that may include:

a. to work with a "non-touching" technique that depends upon the power of the music and the rapport between patient and therapist to accomplish other goals.

b. to find areas of musical involvement that may allow touch through a particular surface, such as the head of a drum, the handle of a mallet, or the surface of a tubular shaker.

If the individual in treatment has trouble discriminating between various surfaces, the music therapist has options that may include:

a. learning to recognize and conceptualize surfaces with musical reinforcement or structure

b. learning to find and identify various hand-held instruments without the using of vision

Instrument and Music Selection

Persons with tactile impairment usually have preferences for certain instruments, e.g., those that would motivate them to make every effort to touch in order to explore or make music. In order to determine preference, the therapist should offer many different instruments from which to choose.

With regard to *tactile defensiveness*, the selection of instruments should be a very individualized search for something that the person in treatment will accept (will touch) in some way that begins to form a link between him/her and another person (the therapist). Possible suggestions include:

1. the surface of a hand drum (either to touch to make sound or to feel sound created on the drum by the music therapist)
2. the surface of an ocean drum (motivated by the sound and/or sight of the metal bearings moving inside)

Physical prompts to promote contact may be necessary in the early stages, in order that the individual may experience the feeling associated with a particular instrument. Once the individual has initiated contact in some way, it would be up to the therapist to build on this relationship, i.e., contact for a longer period of time or more involved contact, etc.

With regard to ***loss of tactile discrimination***, choice of instruments might be based upon personal preferences, but they could also be chosen for their particular function in the therapeutic process. In our experience, this skill is most often addressed with persons who also have visual impairment. Possible suggestions include:

1. smaller instruments that may be identified by touch (out of sight or without vision) by person in treatment
2. certain keys on the piano may be "labeled" with a raised surface in the same way that some buttons on the accordion are modified

Tactile skills play a less important role in communication than the skills of vision and hearing; however, since this ability does provide additional information to each individual, especially in the area of **receptive** communication, it deserves consideration by those who wish to explore all avenues of possible intervention.

The selection of music for either category (**defensiveness** or **discrimination**) may be categorized in one of the following areas:

1. music chosen for its documented properties of *relaxation*, or chosen because of individual preferences (for some, a slow and peaceful *Nocturne* and for others the music of a "heavy-metal" band)
2. music that is *motivating*, usually based upon individual preference
3. music that is *stimulative* to assist in desensitization or to reinforce identification (a Sousa march, a Dixieland band, or some lively renditions of hip-hop artists)

ACCOMMODATIONS

Placement (positioning of the body and/or the instrument used) will probably, in most instances, not be critical; however, as in all situations, it is important that the individual in treatment be comfortable and not distracted by anything that provides more negative input to his/her sense of touch.

Electronic switches connected to devices that ring bells, play drums, and make music in other ways sometimes provide persons with tactile impairment the opportunity to participate.

Clinical example: Cynthia, diagnosed with severe mental retardation and attention deficit disorder (without hyperactivity), was referred to music therapy at age thirty. She had been in a residential facility for most of her life but was now living at home with her mother. Some behavioral problems (non-compliance and tantrums) at home had prompted her mother to seek help.

Cynthia would join the therapist in singing (without much reference to pitch) a few familiar songs (Kum-Ba-Ya, Coming Round the Mountain, etc.). She would play various rhythm instruments (without much reference to a beat), but never with any great degree of enthusiasm.

Much of the time, she would avoid eye contact with the therapist (an older male), and she would refuse or withdraw quickly from any person to person physical contact such as a simple handshake. For several weeks, the therapist accepted this boundary and concentrated on the strategies in which she would participate.

On one occasion, the therapist brought a set of "Boomwhackers" (plastic tubes cut to specific pitches). Seated in front of Cynthia, he demonstrated the technique of hitting the soft tubes on the knees to create sound. She did not seem too impressed but participated by making a few sounds of her own. At one point, the therapist reached out and tapped one of Cynthia's "boomwhackers" with one of his own, and her reaction was one of *great joy!* They continued this exchange for a few minutes, interrupted only by her giggles. During this interlude, Cynthia had experienced touching another person (through the plastic tubes) in a way that was to her safe and entirely acceptable. This incident was a breakthrough in her relationship with the therapist. In future sessions, she asked for the "Boomwhackers," and her enthusiasm continued. At last report, she was still refusing to shake hands, but her level of participation had improved greatly.

As stated previously, treatment of tactile defensiveness was not the primary focus of the work between Cynthia and the therapist; however, it became the key to improvement in other areas that they explored.

Music Therapy for Persons with Language Impairment

When a person has difficulty understanding or reproducing symbols (verbal or non-verbal) in organized patterns required for effective communication, that person may be diagnosed with language impairment and may require therapy to facilitate improvement in this area. A professional music therapist might be asked to provide musical strategies that are complementary to the work of communication therapy (the primary therapy for this sort of disorder). There are at least two categories of language impairment:

1. impairment regarding the language of the home environment during the developmental years
2. impairment in a second language which needs to be learned and understood as quickly as possible in a new environment

One test used by speech-language pathologists to assess language development is the Receptive/Expressive Emergent Language Scale (REEL) (Bzoch & League, 1982). This test produces a language age score for individuals functioning within the developmental period of one to thirty-six months. It is usually applied to the language of the home environment, since early intervention is critical to development of these skills. A child or an adult who finds it necessary to function in a second language might experience language impairment. In this instance the music therapist could be very helpful in providing strategies targeted to improve certain concepts and word usage (Boyd, 1985).

Instrument and Music Selection

Instruments chosen for this type of intervention would take into account the age of the person in treatment, instrumental preferences, and possibly certain ethnic and cultural considerations. Examples include:

1. instruments that are easily accessible to children and possibly those that have "built-in" elements of language (such as a set of shakers in the shapes of apples, oranges, bananas, etc.)
2. instruments that allow increased motion, tactile stimulation, and the imitation of certain accents and rhythms associated with language skills (such as paddle drums and temple blocks)
3. instruments that have historical significance in the language being addressed (such as African drums, maracas, claves, and the guiro)

Music would be chosen largely because of its relationship to the particular language skills being addressed. Preferences should be taken into account. Examples would include:

1. songs and dances from the culture represented by the primary language of the individual in treatment
2. songs based upon age, physical/mental capabilities, and the specific needs of the person in treatment
3. songs from the native language that lend themselves to translation to the language that is the focus of treatment
4. songs that incorporate the use of instruments to improve the possibility of kinetic enhancement of learning

Clinical example: Juan was a seven-year-old with attention deficit disorder, whose family relocated from Mexico to Texas when he was three years old. In the home, Spanish was the language of choice, and his parents had learned enough English to be employed and to function in the community. Unfortunately, Juan and his siblings received very little language training from their parents.

In spite of the lack of training at home, Juan's older siblings adapted well to the classes that were offered in the public schools, which, because of a large influx of new families from south of the border, had developed some good programs to help children make the adjustment.

Learning English seemed to be more of a mystery for Juan, and by the time he reached second grade, he was falling behind his classmates because of his problems with the language. Juan was first referred to a speech-language pathologist, who determined that he had problems with articulation or in understanding the meaning of individual words in English. His difficulties seemed to lie in the areas of paying attention, combining words into intelligible sentences, and in understanding sentences that were spoken to him.

Juan was then referred to a contract music therapist who was bi-lingual. She discovered that in his native language, he was very bright and expressive. Intervention began with work on songs that Juan knew in his native language. These were then translated to English, using the same tune when possible or a new one when needed. To encourage and develop his attention to task, the music therapist used many songs that incorporated movement and rhythm instruments as reinforcers. After about a year of individual sessions with the music therapist, Juan's grades improved, and he was ready to continue in classroom experience with confidence.

In the example above, it may appear that the music therapist was working in a manner similar to a music educator—teaching songs and encouraging the child to learn through the medium of music. This is true to a certain extent, but it was largely because of the special skills of the music therapist that Juan was eventually able to continue on his own. These skills included a working knowledge of both languages, a knowledge of both musical cultures, a knowledge of interventions needed to develop on-task behavior, and a knowledge of the processes involved in language development.

STUDY QUESTIONS FOR CHAPTER 6

1. Music provides another form of communication, especially in area of feelings and _____.
2. Sears (1968) stated that music provides _____, a means of relating to _____ and a means of relating to _____.
3. The initials SLP stand for _____-_____.
4. To the professional educator, **communication** includes the two aspects of SENSORY _____ and BEHAVIORAL _____.
5. The basic skills of communication include _____ SKILLS, _____ SKILLS, and _____ SKILLS.
6. **Visual impairment** may be categorized in four areas: (1) _____, (2) _____, (3) _____, (4) _____.
7. **Hearing impairment** may be categorized in three areas: (1) _____ loss, (2) _____ loss, and (3) _____ loss.
8. **Speech impairment** may be categorized in four areas: (1) _____, (2) _____, (3) _____, and (4) _____.
9. **Tactile (or tactual) impairment** may be categorized in at least four areas: (1) loss of _____, (2) loss of _____, (3) loss of _____ _____, (4) loss of _____.
10. **Language impairment** may be categorized in three major areas: (1) _____, (2) _____, (3) _____.
11. Visual impairment is, for the most part, related to _____ language.
12. The text lists seven ways an individual might identify the flashlight (F), the cymbal (C), and the ball (B). Name four of these.
13. Music therapists not only assist with communication skills. Their intervention helps the individual _____ with his/her present situation.

14. In most music therapy intervention, the songs used should be *age appropriate* and _____ *appropriate.*
15. Is hearing important to *receptive* language? (YES) (NO)
16. Is hearing important to *expressive* language? (YES) (NO)
17. The text offers a simple phrase as a guideline to selection of music for persons with hearing impairment: _____ **is usually more.**
18. An understanding of **basic** sign language may be very important for the professional music therapist. (YES) (NO)
19. There are two types of **tactile impairment.** These are (1) tactile _____ (2) and loss of tactile _____.
20. American sign language is very important in assisting some individuals with (a) expressive language, (b) receptive language, (c) both a and b.

Chapter 7

MUSIC THERAPY AND COGNITIVE SKILLS

- Preliminary Considerations
- Conditions and Causes
- Music Therapy Intervention
- The Role of the Music Therapist

PRELIMINARY CONSIDERATIONS

What are "cognitive" skills? Simply put, these are the skills involved in thinking, in making sense of the world one is in–the skills of **reception** (receiving a stimulus), **perception** (identifying a stimulus), **conception** (ideas about the stimulus), and **memory** (of the stimulus and of your ideas). In short, it is the full operation of the human brain that provides the potential for the individual to fulfill his/her role as a member of society.

Cognitive skills (at any age) are the abilities that an individual has acquired to enable him/her to *access, interpret, modify,* and *retain* information. An infant lying in a crib, who is hitting a rattle suspended at arm's length, is demonstrating the most basic cognitive skills: hearing the sound of the rattle, sorting and comparing that sound to others, and making a decision to repeat the motion to receive the stimulus. This experience may be imprinted in the baby's brain as a type of memory that will allow him/her to repeat this activity in the future and/or modify it to set the stage for more learning and further interaction with the world.

CONDITIONS AND CAUSES

The term "cognitive skill" is sometimes associated with "academic skill" or even "IQ," and for many children difficulties are first noticed in the school environment. Cognitive skills encompass all human brain activity from birth and even during gestation, where research has shown that learning occurs (Redmond, 1989). Music therapists working in the public or private school setting usually encounter children diagnosed with **learning disabilities**. Included under this category is a condition known as attention deficit hyperactivity disorder (ADHD). Attention to requested or required tasks is the primary condition needed for learning to take place, and a disability in this area is sometimes considered to be a behavior disorder. Perceptual problems and other conditions related to brain injury or dysfunction, e.g., dyslexia and developmental aphasia, are also learning disabilities. According to Public Law 94–142, a "free and public education" shall be provided for persons who are mentally retarded, deaf and hard of hearing, speech impaired, seriously emotionally disturbed, orthopedically impaired, and specifically learning disabled (Lathom, 1981, p. 18).

To say that a person has a "learning disability" uses a euphemistic term, which is much kinder than to say that he/she is "mentally retarded." The term also indicates a more specific approach to the person's problems than do words like "retarded" or "intellectually limited." The person's problems, after due assessment, may be seen as a *specific number* of deficits in the area of cognitive skills.

Visual impairments or **hearing impairments** are critical factors in the development of cognitive skills, since they limit the ability of the individual to *access* information.

Impaired motor skills may affect the person who has difficulty with the written word, difficulty traveling to and from places of learning, difficulty reading Braille (if that is a needed option), and difficulty participating in activities that require a large amount of physical involvement.

Developmental disabilities that affect the process of acquiring and refining cognitive skills occur in a chronological sequence, and these changes may impact any or all areas accessing information–visual, aural, tactile, motor, and the ability to process such information. The age and stage of a child in development may make dramatic differences in all skill areas, including cognitive; therefore, this age-based phenomenon must be considered, i.e., is the change related to the normal expected changes in development?

Deficits in cognitive skills may affect older adults, especially those diagnosed with dementia or Alzheimer's disease. Other conditions such as depression and reactions to some prescribed medications may affect one's cognitive ability. Persons at any age, who have suffered trauma and neurological damage as the result of an accident or other situations, may also experience cognitive difficulties, such as organizing their thoughts and regaining mental abilities.

It is important to remember that a deficit in any skill area, including those discussed in previous chapters and the chapters that follow, may be part of the equation in considering problems that affect cognitive functioning. The central nervous system forms the "powerhouse" of all human activity and affects all other systems and is, likewise, affected by them.

MUSIC THERAPY INTERVENTION

Professional music therapists work with persons within a wide range of disabilities, and, as stated before, the diagnosis does not always determine the type of treatment. Assessment of specific problems is the key to determining whether the skill most needed at a particular time is "cognitive" in general terms or sometimes more specifically called "pre-academic," such as attention deficit skills, motor skills, communication skills, and/or social-emotional skills. If the needs of the individual are specific cognitive deficits such as perception and organization of stimuli, these may need to be addressed before direct attention is given to the areas of formal academic learning.

In the Learning Environment

Music therapists working in the schools usually work very closely with classroom teachers. In many systems, their work takes on the role of a consultant, and they are expected to offer suggestions and plans for music activities that may be implemented by the teacher (as a kind of "practicing" of skills) following a demonstration by the music therapist. When special problems arise that cannot be treated in this way, the music therapist may be called upon to develop a more individualized program for the child or children who most need this service. Some of the disabling conditions of children that may affect cognitive functioning, and which the music therapist may encounter in the learning environment, are as follows:

1. **attention deficit hyperactive disorder** (ADHD)–characterized by lack of attention to tasks, plus hyperactivity, and impulsiveness–usually appearing in the early years of development but sometimes undiagnosed until adulthood–originally called attention

deficit disorder (ADD), which does not include hyperactivity but only distraction from on-task behavior and perhaps disconnection or "dreaming" behavior

2. **auditory discrimination disorder**–characterized by the inability to hear and distinguish similarities and differences between sounds, e.g., high–low, soft–loud

3. **auditory memory disorder**–characterized by the inability to retain and recall significant segments of sound

4. **auditory sequencing disorder**–characterized by the inability to retain and repeat rhythms and to integrate these into patterns of speech

5. **Down syndrome**–characterized by mental retardation and physical abnormalities, resulting from a genetic defect

6. **Rett's syndrome**–characterized by physical disabilities, speech impairment, and severe mental retardation

7. **traumatic brain injury**–characterized by serious deficits in cognitive functioning resulting from an accident or other cause.

Clinical example: Billy, ten years old, was observed in a classroom setting, where he was frequently out of his seat during the time that others were engaged in completing assignments. He was either distracted by his own thoughts or by other students. Many tasks did not interest him at all, and when he did participate, his on-task behavior was minimal. His reading skills were well below grade level, and cognitive (or academic) development was at risk.

When asked what he was supposed to be doing at any given moment, he frequently did not seem to know. It was determined that he seemed to be unable to properly process and repeat instructions that were given to him by the teacher. This deficit in *auditory sequencing* was a "pre-academic" behavior that needed to be addressed before learning could occur.

The music therapist began to work with Billy in a small group where percussion instruments were used in a "call-response" fashion. In a pretest, Billy could only imitate one or two simple patterns of sound. As he developed interest in this activity, the therapist increased the length and complexity of the rhythm patterns. Eventually, a posttest showed that he had greatly improved his ability to repeat patterns given to him. During individual sessions, Billy began to transfer rhythm patterns to speech. The therapist used sentences modeled after instructions given in the classroom.

After Billy had demonstrated that he could repeat the instructions given by the teacher, it was time to address the original problem noted in the referral to music therapy. After a few sessions, a baseline was formulated regarding his on-task behavior.

The music therapist began composing songs to assist (and reward) Billy with his assigned reading. At this point, his learning behaviors (the reason for the original referral) were being addressed directly. The structure of the music was gradually lengthened to help him remain on task for longer periods of time.

Subsequent protocols required Billy to successfully perform his tasks without music in order to be allowed to listen to favorite songs as a reward for completing his assignment. Once he could stay on task for longer periods of time, he began to benefit from the classroom instruction (Michel, 1983).

In the Pre-Academic Clinical Environment

When cognitive skills are slow to develop during the early years of life, an individual may be referred to a music therapist for evaluation. The principal problems addressed may include communication and motor skills, which were discussed in a previous chapter, and social-emotional skills, which will be discussed in the chapter that follows.

Clinical example: Daniel, four years old and diagnosed with apraxia (inability to voluntarily move muscles related to articulation) and attention deficit hyperactive disorder, was referred to the music therapist by his communication therapist in hopes of finding other interventions to complement her own. Considering his age, he seemed to understand most of what was said to him (in the therapeutic and home environments), but his expressive language was a combination of gestures and "shrieks"–the latter usually indicating his pleasure with a particular activity.

During the initial session a lot of time was devoted to physically managing his desire to run to and from various instruments in the room. His "shrieks" indicated that he enjoyed many types of music stimuli, but none of these seemed to capture his attention for more than thirty seconds. Goals were established to help him make progress in the areas of communication skills and attention to task.

A breakthrough occurred in the third session when a song was sung about the therapist's blue and gray walking shoes. Daniel responded with "boo," which was the first real vowel sound heard in this setting. When the word "up" was paired with a glissando on the piano, he got very excited and responded with the word "up." This was eventually paired with throwing a ball in the air, and "down" was added when the ball was thrown on the floor. His first two-syllable word was "music"–in response to a song introduced by the therapist. This accomplishment brought tears to his mother's eyes, because he had never been able to articulate the word "mama."

At this point in the therapeutic process, Daniel's attention to task had shown no improvement. The therapy room had no windows, and during one session, he discovered that a quick trip to the light switch would create a temporary "blackout." In the next session, the music therapist placed a small lamp in another part of the room to maintain a safe environment, but Daniel's trips to the light switch continued. Another breakthrough in on-task behavior occurred when the therapist devised a "light show," which was conducted in total darkness with two "light sticks" (a la *Star Wars*). During sessions that followed, Daniel was offered the light show as a reward for his staying in his chair and participating in the other activities. His on-task behavior immediately increased to one minute.

When Daniel was ten years old, individual services were terminated in favor of group activities offered through the special education department in his public school. He was still behind his peers in terms of cognitive (academic) development, but his vocabulary had increased dramatically, and his on-task behavior was approaching ten minutes (Pinson, 1991).

In the Institutional Environment

Music therapists working in public and private facilities for persons with developmental disabilities and for children in crisis encounter a unique set of diagnoses and circumstances, which can be very challenging (and very rewarding) to the therapist. In addition to the cognitive conditions mentioned previously, special problems include the following:

1. **behavior disorder**–characterized by inappropriate behaviors which interfere with the developmental process
2. **conduct disorder**–characterized by aggression, destruction, and overt violations of social norms
3. **epilepsy**–characterized by "seizures," during which the individual experiences momentary loss of motor functions, sometimes accompanied by violent shaking and incontinence
4. **oppositional defiant disorder**–characterized by negative and hostile behaviors that impede functioning
5. **posttraumatic stress disorder**–characterized by recurring memories of stressful situations, originally associated with persons engaged in military combat but also experienced by persons who are victims of accidents or abuse.

Clinical example: Charlotte, age 18 and diagnosed with mild mental retardation, epilepsy, and a behavior disorder, was referred to the music therapist when a caregiver noticed that she enjoyed singing along with the radio. She had been a resident of a state facility for persons with developmental disabilities since age eight, when her behavior became unmanageable in her home environment.

When the music therapist first met Charlotte, she was dressed in an institutional "gown," because she had destroyed the clothes given to her by her family. Her general appearance indicated that she had no interest in grooming, and her facial expression was one of sadness and defeat; however, she was happy to discover that the therapist could play some of the songs she liked to sing. When she sang, demonstrating good pitch and rhythm, she smiled occasionally. During the initial session, the therapist recorded six petit mal seizures—each lasting only a few seconds and characterized by disorientation and mild loss of motor control. At the end of the first session, Charlotte refused to leave the music therapy room, and it was ultimately necessary to use restraint and to call for an escort to take her back to her residence.

Training in academic skills for Charlotte had been terminated because of her disruptive behavior. At the time that she met the music therapist, she could recite the alphabet, count to one hundred, and recognize her name in print. Since special education was no longer offered to her, she spent most days watching television at her residence. (Note: In the state where this occurred, restriction from educational experiences because of behavior is no longer allowed.)

Charlotte's goal in music therapy was to make progress in social-emotional skills. Her objective was to learn to sing songs aimed at improving her self-esteem. During the first several months of therapy, rapport developed between Charlotte and the therapist, her disruptive and manipulative behaviors decreased, and she was able to join the choir and percussion ensemble. By this time, the number of seizures recorded during music therapy (individual and group) was about one per week.

During music therapy activities, her behavior was generally under control, but problems continued at her residence and elsewhere on campus. For this reason, she was not allowed to take trips with the campus groups to perform for community functions. After three more years of involvement and two failed attempts to behave appropriately on trips, she was allowed to travel with the performing groups on a regular basis.

At this point, Charlotte's behavior had improved enough that she could be considered for more cognitive (specifically academic) training, but, unfortunately, at age twenty-two, she was no longer eligible for special education services. The music therapist included some basic reading and writing exercises during sessions, but these were not sufficient to make up for the many years lost because of her other problems.

Charlotte was transferred to a group home in the community, where no music therapy services were provided. Her original behaviors resurfaced, and she was eventually returned to the institution where she still resides.

THE ROLE OF THE MUSIC THERAPIST

Considering this case study, it might appear that the therapist in a public or private institution faces more "roadblocks" than one working in other settings. This is not necessarily the case. Many elements of care are more predictable in the institution than in some home environments. Proper diet and medical services are always available, and if the institution employs a model of a "treatment team," the outcome of therapy may actually be more predictable than in "less-restrictive" settings.

In *all* therapeutic environments, there are always situations in the life of the individual in treatment that are *totally* outside the control of the therapist. The role of the professional music therapist is to use his/her knowledge and skills in the most effective and efficient way possible. If this is done, the therapist can experience a sense of accomplishment, even though the actual outcome of therapy may be dependent upon numerous factors related to the individual served that are not necessarily a part of the therapeutic process.

STUDY QUESTIONS FOR CHAPTER 7

1. Define "cognitive skills."
2. Give an example of a very basic cognitive skill (during infancy).
3. The term "cognitive skill" is sometimes associated with _____.
4. According to Public Law 94–142 are there disabilities that are *not* included in the category known as **learning disabilities**?
5. Are cognitive skills a problem only for children in the early developmental years, or do they affect persons at other stages of life? Explain.
6. Define: attention deficit hyperactive disorder, auditory discrimination disorder, auditory memory disorder, auditory sequencing disorder.
7. In the case study of Billy, what behavior had to be addressed before he could make progress in the area of cognitive (academic) skills?
8. What strategy did the therapist use to help Billy improve his on-task behavior? How was it modified for adaptation to a classroom situation?
9. Daniel was referred to music therapy by the communication therapist, whose focus was the development of speech. What other behavior was also addressed during sessions with the music therapist?

10. What was Daniel's first two-syllable word?
11. How did the music therapist take an unwanted behavior and turn it into a reward for on-task behavior?
12. How is a **behavior disorder** different from a **conduct disorder**?
13. Is **posttraumatic stress disorder** only associated with persons involved in military combat?
14. Why was Charlotte denied special education services in the institution? Is this practice still in effect today in the state where she lives?
15. If Charlotte had been given special education services while her behavior was unmanageable, is it likely that much learning would have occurred?
16. Is the problem of factors beyond the control of the therapist unique to the institutional setting, or are such problems encountered in most settings?

Chapter 8

MUSIC THERAPY AND
SOCIAL-EMOTIONAL SKILLS

- Preliminary Considerations
- Conditions
- Individual Social-Emotional Skills
- Group Social-Emotional Skills
- Music Therapy Intervention

PRELIMINARY CONSIDERATIONS

Social skills are generally defined as learned behaviors that affect interpersonal relationships and the individual's relation to society as a whole. **Emotional skills** are defined as learned behaviors that allow expressions of individual feelings. These skills are usually grouped together, because they seem be acquired during the developmental stages in tandem or simultaneously. Everyone at times experiences feelings and emotions apart from interpersonal involvement, but the influence of social factors is always present. The emotions of the most isolated individual may also be directly affected by the *absence* of social interaction.

Children by nature tend to experience feelings and emotions as being more self-centered, because they are relatively unaware of the impact and importance of social relationships. Awareness is acquired as they develop and usually peaks during adolescence, when self-centeredness struggles with the concept of accepting oneself as a member of the human race.

Attitudes usually develop *slowly*, so change is also a *slow* process. Attitudes are reflected in the actions of individuals, which can be measured in behavioral terms. Thought processes, along with emotions, affect the development of attitudes. Attitudes are in many cases learned "positions" which condition responses to many events encountered by an individual. They are acquired from experiences of the individual. Reactions of others may lead to modification of attitudes.

ATTITUDES= thoughts + feelings + events

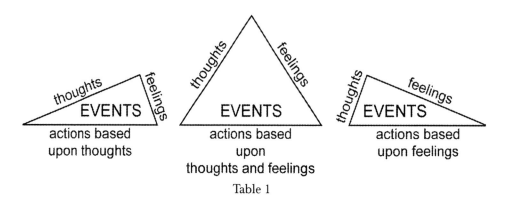

| actions based upon thoughts | actions based upon thoughts and feelings | actions based upon feelings |

Table 1

Social-emotional skills, with the possible exception of those affected by psychoses, brain damage, or substance abuse, are learned behavioral responses to events, usually involving interaction with other persons, which are both reflexive and thoughtful. If they are thoughtful, it usually indicates that an individual has developed a measure of self-control. Table 2 shows how self-control plays a role in responses to social-emotional events and situations. As children **we think**, **we feel**, and **we act** accordingly (either appropriately or inappropriately). Some children (and adults) lack the ability to insert an element of self-control into the equation. Like attitudes, **self-control** develops very slowly, and if self-control is lacking in an individual, acquiring this skill may be a long and tedious process. Self-control is a **filter** that may prevent thoughts and

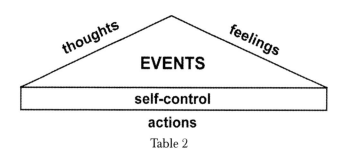

Table 2

feelings from erupting into behaviors that are not appropriate. Acquiring this skill can also improve a person's ability to process and organize information that is not directly related to social-emotional behavior.

CONDITIONS

In the area of social-emotional skills, it may be helpful to divide these into three categories of functioning. Some individuals will have what is known as a "dual diagnosis" in which more than one condition is contributing to the distress. The three basic categories are as follows:

I. Physical–Neurological

Alzheimer's disease–characterized by deterioration of all cognitive functioning followed by loss of control of all bodily functions

Asperger's disorder–characterized by normal intelligence, splinter skills, and highly expressive language–and sometimes accompanied by autistic like behaviors and poor social skills

Autism–characterized by ritualistic behaviors, destructive behaviors, dysfunctional self-absorption, preoccupation with inanimate objects, and tactile defensiveness

Dementia–characterized by a deterioration in memory, judgement, abstract thinking, and problem solving skills

Developmental disability–characterized by lack of development in all skill areas that begin at birth or in early childhood

II. Psychological–Behavioral

Anxiety disorder–characterized by unrealistic or excessive anxiety, panic attacks, or avoidance behavior

Behavior disorder–characterized by problems in relating to others which interfere with social-emotional skills and learning

Conduct disorder–characterized by breaking social norms, including aggression toward others and destruction of property

Delusions–characterized by a set of invalid beliefs that usually have no basis in reality

Juvenile delinquency–characterized by lack of or distortion of social-emotional skills which are clearly in violation of the law

Mood disorder–characterized by a disturbance in mood which could significantly interfere with everyday functioning.

III. Psychoses and Neuroses

Schizophrenia–characterized by periods of alteration of thinking, perception, affect, emotional responses, and behavior (psychosis)

Personality disorder–characterized by demonstrations of extreme and inflexible behaviors that cause difficulties in all areas of functioning (neurosis)

Sociopathic disorder–characterized by significant alienation from others, manipulation of others, and sometimes dangerous behaviors toward other persons (neurosis)

Bi-polar disorder–characterized by periods of extreme depression and elation and often has a physiological basis (may be neurosis or psychosis)

INDIVIDUAL SOCIAL-EMOTIONAL SKILLS

What does a person think and do in the absence of peers? Even in an individual music therapy session, there is the element of *control* that may be absent when a person has to face situations all alone. At these moments, each individual may be very vulnerable, and the job of the therapist may be that of helping such a person develop social-emotional skills necessary for survival during such difficult times.

Except for "psychotic" episodes, acts of rage, and/or situations where lack or loss of developmental milestones (skills) is a factor, much negative behavior may manifest itself in a thought process. There are individual reactions to stimuli that occur "automatically," but many other self-defeating and self-destructive **behaviors** are the result of one's thinking, and they may be the product of **erroneous choices**. For some individuals, such choices may in some cases follow negative thinking and/or deprivation and result in inappropriate behaviors.

The diagram that follows suggests the process in which negative thoughts and thinking may result in problem conditions and behaviors. These categories are not exclusive, i.e., they may be combined with those from other columns, but it is a general overview of some of the problems that professional music therapists may encounter. It should be noted that any condition on the list could also possibly be the symptoms of some undiscovered medical condition.

In suggesting the connections between thinking and behavior in the diagram, we realize that, although much research has contributed to knowledge in these areas, there are no absolute theories that point to a clear and unquestioned relationship.

SITUATION *(stress)*	CONDITION *(distress)*	RESPONSE *(disorder)*
negative thoughts about self and others	poor self-esteem, lack of energy, depression, anxiety, lack of motivation, inability to concentrate	neglect of self care, truancy, chemical/drug/alcohol abuse, behavior disorder, neglect of environment, eating disorders, self-injury
deprivation or distortion of physical and/or social needs	grandiose feelings, physical dysfunction, delusions, sleep disorders, compulsive thinking	deviant behaviors, criminal activity, addictions (drugs, alcohol, television, internet, or food) suicidal tendencies, paranoia, conduct disorder

SOCIAL-EMOTIONAL SKILLS IN GROUPS

As mentioned before, in the group situation (and even one-to-one with a music therapist), there is introduced an element of *control* by the presence of another person or persons that will probably have an influence on the ability of the individual to make **decisions**. This is not to say that the decisions made in this context will always be positive, but in the presence of others, dramatic outbursts of emotion, destruction of property, and aggression are less likely to occur.

In working with groups, the music therapist must become aware of the *antecedents* which may trigger inappropriate *behaviors*. Here is a partial list based upon the experience of the authors.

ANTECEDENTS	BEHAVIORS
requests from therapist that require compliance	unwillingness to share instruments and/or materials, unwillingness to take turns, carelessness with instruments and/or materials, desire to "take charge"
comments perceived as negative from therapist or other other members of group	threats to others, physical aggression, hypersensitivity, mood swings, defiance of authority, attention getting, decreased ability in coordination, destruction of instruments and/or materials, decreased perceptual ability

MUSIC THERAPY INTERVENTION

Improved social-emotional skills in the group setting may enable the individual in treatment to take some steps toward greater **personal responsibility** in social settings. In one-to-one sessions and group activities, the professional music therapist will devise goals that assist in developing skills such as:

1. improved confidence and less anxiety about musical performance
2. improved optimism and less depressing thoughts about the outcome of future events
3. improved sensitivity to the feelings and needs of others
4. improved compliance with expectations of the therapist and of the community at large
5. improved skills of social interaction

Individual sessions sometimes provide a good opportunity for the music therapist to have a positive impact upon a person who needs to improve social-emotional skills; however, this more intense involvement may also bring into play new and different situations that demand careful attention from the therapist, such as:

Transference and **countertransference**, terms normally associated with psychoanalysis, may possibly surface in individual relationships with persons who lack appropriate social-emotional skills, because some of these individuals (including therapists) may have emotional needs that move them in the direction of these types of relationships.

Transference occurs when an individual in treatment unconsciously projects relationships which he/she has experienced with others directly to the therapist. When there is **countertransference** in the relationship, it means that the therapist is unconsciously projecting his/her feelings and behaviors about others *directly* to the person in treatment. Either of these situations may develop in a therapeutic encounter, and music therapists must make every effort to be aware of them, since they do not represent the ideal interpersonal relationship between therapist and the person in treatment. Unless recognized and dealt with, such projections usually make progress more difficult; therefore, the professional music therapist should continually evaluate the type of relationship that is developed in one-to-one treatment. The concentric circle in Chapter 1 illustrates this process.

Clinical example: Edward, age 22, was originally hospitalized for what was described as "strange behavior" following his discharge from military service. He would emit a loud "roar" at unpredictable intervals and for no apparent cause. He was referred to music therapy, because it was known that he was a very accomplished pianist.

In the first few sessions a "therapeutic relationship" was developed as Edward played piano accompaniments while the therapist played the violin. In this musical environment, the "strange behavior" was almost non-existent, but it was discovered that music for Edward was a "fantasy world" in which he found escape from reality. The music therapist set up musical ensembles in which Edward could expand his social experiences while maintaining "safety" as he perceived it.

Over a period of twelve or fourteen months, Edward's ability to relate to others in a positive way improved considerably, and he was given more grounds privileges–allowing him to leave his ward and return without an escort. He was given privileges that would allow him to visit relatives, but he declined this opportunity.

At this point in the treatment, the music therapist left the hospital to take a position elsewhere. Edward became very upset, retreated to his world of fantasy, and the "strange behaviors" surfaced again. Becoming aware of this turn of events, the therapist contacted Edward's brother and discussed the treatment that had shown such promising results up to this time.

The brother, who was also a violinist, had Edward transferred to a hospital near his home and initiated regular visits. Music became a catalyst for reestablishing their relationship, which had been terminated when Edward entered military service. At last report, Edward was making good progress toward return to society (Michel, 1985).

The example above presents several possibilities for development of **transference** and **countertransference** in the relationship, e.g., the therapist, who played the violin as did the patient's brother, could have set the stage for displacement of the patient's feelings (transference) from childhood to the therapist. The therapist also had a brother and had developed ways of interacting with him that might have been transferred to the patient (countertransference). Neither transference nor countertransference occurred in this therapeutic relationship, and this was in part due to the fact that the therapist had a good understanding about the background of the patient. This knowledge was also a key to treatment that eventually continued in another setting.

If the behavior of an individual is "out of control" to the point that he/she is dangerous to others, it is probably not a good idea to involve that person in certain types of group activities. In the next case study, the behavior of the individual initially only allowed one-to-one sessions, and for a time, even these were not possible. The group became an option when his behavior was under better control.

Clinical example: Ernie, age 20, diagnosed with mild mental retardation and a conduct disorder, was referred to the music therapist by the psychologist assigned to monitor his case. He had been cursing, aggressing toward peers and staff, and refusing to go to work. It was noted that he sang and danced with music on the radio and played rhythms with his hands on the furniture.

Because of his aggressive behaviors, the music therapist first began visiting Ernie at his residence. Good rapport was established during the music sessions, and although Ernie displayed no hostility or aggression toward the therapist, behaviors of this type continued at other times during the week.

As the music therapist arrived one day, Ernie was moving about the living room, shouting and cursing and threatening one of the attendants with a baseball bat that he was swinging in the air. The music therapist was drafted to become part of a three-man team to "disarm" Ernie. Two of the attendants were able to restrain him, while the music therapist retrieved the baseball bat.

Shortly after this very dangerous, life-threatening incident, the medical team agreed to increase drug therapy in an effort to control these outbursts. The next time the music therapist visited with Ernie, he was receiving large doses of lithium, which reduced him to a person who walked about slowly saying very little and displaying none of the positive musical behaviors noted originally. His affect was blunt, and his former expressive personality was absent. At this time, music therapy services were discontinued, because it was felt that Ernie was too "out of touch" to benefit from strategies developed by the music therapist.

Over a period of several months, the doses of lithium were reduced to the point that allowed Ernie's personality, affect, and positive musical behaviors to return with only a few isolated instances of hostility and aggression. Ernie was able to return to work, and because of this schedule, it was impossible to continue individual music therapy sessions.

The treatment team agreed that Ernie's aggressive behaviors were controlled sufficiently to allow him to participate in the choir and percussion ensemble, which met after hours. In these groups, his natural musical abilities gave him a new sense of pride in himself. His peers admired his abilities, and audiences that responded to performances of the ensembles gave him an even bigger "boost." Although there were a few "tense moments" when Ernie displayed some discontent with authority and with some of the comments made by peers, it was possible to redirect him to more music activities to prevent a return of his aggression. He began assuming responsibility for handling equipment for the ensemble and for escorting (with supervision) persons with severe physical disabilities to the music therapy area. His drug regimen had been reduced to minimal dosage, and he continued to display "gentlemanly" behavior (Pinson, 1980).

The example above demonstrates the effectiveness of music therapy in providing a positive climate for accomplishment and acceptance, which may help individuals with behavior problems learn new ways of expressing their feelings and frustrations. It also demonstrates the importance of teamwork in providing a balanced regimen of medication and therapy to assist in rehabilitation. Not all persons who display hostility and aggressive behaviors respond this well to medication or to music therapy, but it is a "feather in the cap" of our profession when it occurs.

It is possible that the description of "strange" behaviors, hostility, and aggression may leave the reader less than interested in the field of music therapy. It is important to understand that in many music therapy settings, these behaviors are practically non-existent, and when they are present, they represent only a small percentage of persons in treatment. Dealing with difficult behaviors is a significant challenge for music therapists, and many therapists find that aspect of the work very exciting and fulfilling.

It should be noted that the development of social-emotional skills is a *continuum* that begins in infancy. The **Music Therapy Assessment Profile** (MTAP, Michel & Rohrbacher, 1983) lists some of these early developmental milestones. Below is a partial list of these skills:

> 0–2 months: quiets when picked up, quiets to friendly face or voice, quiets to singing or music, smiles or vocalizes to talk or touch
>
> 3–5 months: smiles or vocalizes to mirror image of self, recognizes and responds to familiar people, discriminates strangers in room
>
> 6–8 months: seeks personal attention and holds out arms to be picked up, prefers to be with people, explores features of a familiar person
>
> 9–11 months: cries, screams (or otherwise communicates displeasure) when music is withdrawn and to attract attention
>
> 12–15 months: greets verbally (says "hello" or "goodbye"), responds differently to young children
>
> 16–19 months: plays musical instrument apart from familiar person for five minutes

ADDENDUM TO CHAPTER 8–MICHEL

The causes for inappropriate behaviors or lack of adequate skills to deal with social and emotional problems may be very complex. It is not our purpose to minimize the importance of trying to determine under-lying causes. There is always the possibility of medical causes such as autism, Asperger's disorder, cerebral palsy, other types of brain damage, or disorders of unknown origin.

If a medical diagnosis is given as a cause of the individual's problems and a limiting factor in their possible solution, it will be important for the therapist to have this information. The music therapy assessment will focus primarily on the social and emotional skills observed or as measured by tools such as the MTAP, but good background informa-tion is critical to the success of the protocol that is developed and the theory on which it is based.

Beginning with adolescence the social-emotional skills required of each individual become even more complicated, and problems at this stage and later in life may be the result of unresolved conflicts or un-learned skills. At each stage of life medical diagnoses must be "ruled out" or accounted for as causal before treatment protocols can be developed.

How do people change? This is a question that is continually asked by all persons including music therapists. It is not as simple as getting people to think "straight" or "correctly," and one can never assume that a person will become aware of his/her need and take the necessary steps to change. One of the most used theories of counseling today is one that takes into consideration the cognitive aspect of behavior, i.e., what people think may well be causal or related in some way to their behavior. This theory is called **cognitive-behavioral** to recognize both aspects of skills in the social and emotional as well as cognitive areas and the difficulty of providing therapy that helps the individual to learn to change from both standpoints.

How is music used in effecting such change? Music therapy groups composed of persons with similar problems offer the participants the opportunity to "play out" behaviors—a process that requires complete attention and cooperation from those involved. As mentioned previ-ously, even in one-to-one encounters, the therapist and the person in treatment may form a "group" of their own in which activities of this type are pursued. Remember that the music therapist must always be *accountable* for the protocol developed. This means taking data to record progress or lack of same.

It should be recognized that much of the behavior of individuals (all of us!) is *not* always preceded by conscious thought but, in many instances, occurs in an "automatic" way. Our playing of musical instruments is often done in this way, and driving a car sometimes becomes so habitual that we forget to observe the rules of safety. Some forms of this type of "thoughtless" behavior, which is called "impulsive" (implying being out of control), can be very negative and destructive.

Music therapists may be able to help individuals who suffer the consequences of non-thinking, unconscious behaviors by attempting to get them to realize, i.e., think about the problems and assist them in learning new, more appropriate social-emotional skills. This might be done through musical dramatization in a therapy group or through special songs that teach an individual new skills and which provide the opportunity for "homework." The learning of music itself, such as playing an instrument, demands thoughtful, focused behavior, which may be generalized to other aspects of life to enhance coping skills in social-emotional situations.

AND FURTHERMORE–PINSON

Additionally, it is important to realize that the medium of music is a natural unifying force, and in the context of music making individuals often become so absorbed that their inappropriate behaviors take a back seat to the beauty of the moment. The **triangle** (Chapter 1) demonstrates the *stability* and *structure*, which are inherent and extremely valuable in music therapy.

Even the structure and stability of society (local and global) are strengthened when people engage in sharing music. During the cold war between Russia and the United States, when very little was occurring at the diplomatic level, both countries were sharing music through cultural exchange. The effects of this "mass music therapy" can never be adequately measured, but it was probably an important factor in the eventual re-establishment of peaceful relations.

An important branch of music therapy that addresses social and emotional problems is known as Guided Imagery and Music (GIM). It is "a technique in which the act of listening to classical music is combined with a relaxed state of mind and body in order to evoke imagery for the purpose of self-actualization" (Summer, 1988). Imagery usually reflects aspects of self and is used by individuals, with the aid of a GIM-trained therapist, to foster positive growth and resolution of difficult situations.

It is important to note that GIM is "only useful with those populations in which the client (1) is capable of symbolic thinking, (2) can differentiate between symbolic thinking and reality, (3) can relate his/her experience to the therapist, and (4) can achieve positive growth as a result" (Summer, 1988).

STUDY QUESTIONS FOR CHAPTER 8

1. Define **social skills**. Define **emotional skills**. Why are they usually grouped together in describing the way an individual functions?
2. Attitudes = _____ + _____ + _____.
3. Attitudes develop _____ and, consequently, when change is necessary, it is usually a _____ process.
4. As children we _____, we _____, we _____ accordingly (either appropriately or inappropriately).
5. As adults, we must develop an element of _____–_____.
6. In the text, Alzheimer's disease, Asperger's disorder, autism, dementia, and developmental disability are under the general category of _____–_____. You should be familiar with the definitions of each of these conditions.
7. In the text, anxiety disorder, behavior disorder, conduct disorder, delusions, juvenile offenders, and mood disorder are under the general category of _____–_____. You should be familiar with the definitions of each of these disorders.
8. In the text, schizophrenia, personality disorder, sociopathic disorder, and bi-polar disorder are under the general category of _____ – _____. You should be familiar with the definitions of these disorders.
9. Many self-_____ and even self-_____ behaviors are the result of **erroneous decisions**.
10. What two types of life situations may trigger the bad decisions mentioned in the preceding question?
    (1) negative thoughts about _____ and _____.
    (2) Deprivation or distortion of _____ and _____ needs.
11. Does the presence of a music therapist constitute a "group"?
12. Why are **better decisions** more possible in a group therapy situation?
13. Define **transference**.
14. Define **countertransference**.
15. What was the "strange behavior" that Edward was displaying?
16. If music was a "fantasy world" for Edward, how could it possibly be a medium for treatment? Think ISO Principle.

17. Are instances of hostility and aggression part of the everyday life of most music therapists? If not, why not?
18. If you decide to not study for the next quiz, that is an erroneous decision.
19. What do the initials "GIM" stand for? Describe this technique briefly.

Chapter 9

PROFESSIONAL ETHICS AND DISCLOSURE

- Preliminary Considerations
- Ethics and Disclosure Defined
- Examples of Ethical Violations

PRELIMINARY CONSIDERATIONS

It would seem that in the noble profession of music therapy, generally composed of persons with high ideals and a desire to serve others, there would be no room for anything except the most upright and ethical behavior. Certainly the **personal responsibility** that we expect from the persons we treat starts "at home."

In spite of the high degree of character and responsibility among music therapists, there are some inherent "pitfalls" in our practice that lend themselves to the possibility of unethical behavior. These may be generally described as follows:

1. There is much misunderstanding about the "healing" powers of music, and if the professional music therapist does not "self-regulate," the public we serve may be led to believe that there is more "magic" in our process than is actually the case. Unless it is counterproductive to treatment, we must always be careful to *disclose* our true feelings regarding the possible outcomes of our intervention, based upon scientific principles and research in our field, as well as personal professional experience.

2. Many of the persons we serve are *unable* to make a personal assessment of their own progress (or lack of same), and without an

advocate to assist, they are very vulnerable to therapists who continue to offer treatment when it is no longer needed, or when it is less than effective.

3. Professional music therapists are sometimes tempted to speak or act negatively regarding the work of non-professionals who use music in various ways. Unless these persons are representing themselves as "music therapists," such negativity serves no useful purpose and may make some observers think that we have an attitude of "ownership" of the medium of music, when, in fact, our "ownership" is about how and when it is applied as a valid therapy.

4. Although some music therapists work as part of a treatment team through which their techniques are monitored more closely, many others work without direct supervision. This means that they must always be very careful to report the "facts" or results of their work as objectively as possible.

ETHICS AND DISCLOSURE DEFINED

Ethics may be defined as an attitude that promotes actions that are not selfish, that are good for everyone concerned, that will do no harm to those involved, and that comply with the laws and moral codes of society. **Personal responsibility** based upon good decisions is at the center of ethical conduct and affects the entire life of the individual. **Rotary International**, the world's largest service organization, employs the **Four Way Test** to encourage ethical conduct. If each individual asks these questions of himself/herself before making critical decisions, the results will most likely be a more ethical society.

The Four Way Test
1. Is it the truth?
2. Is it fair to all concerned?
3. Will it build good will and better friendships?
4. Will it be beneficial to all concerned? (Miller, S. 1999)

Each of the organizations that represent the music therapist, the American Music Therapy Association and the Certification Board for Music Therapists, has developed its own **Code of Ethics**.

The **Code of Ethics** of AMTA describes the relationship of the music therapist to the association, to other professionals, to the community,

and to the persons whom he/she serves. It includes professional behaviors, which are discussed further in a document known as the
Standards of Clinical Practice (AMTA, 2003).

In 1998, the **Code of Professional Practice** of CBMT was adopted
in place of a more general Code of Ethics. This document describes the
relationship of the music therapist to the certifying agency. The original
Code of Ethics of CBMT was more like the AMTA document, but since
the primary responsibility of the organization is to monitor certification,
the new Code of Professional Practice is perhaps more appropriate.

You will note that the number of topics covered by AMTA is fairly
lengthy and comprehensive. The CBMT speaks about ethical practice–
but with a focus on the responsibility of the therapist to adhere to all
guidelines regarding certification. AMTA oversees the "profession" *and*
the "practice" of music therapy. The Code of AMTA has been developed over a period of many years, and as new situations develop or
come to the attention of the Association, the document will probably
be expanded and/or modified to cover these.

Robert Kitts (1999), a psychotherapist, has compiled a list of areas in
which the ethical conduct of a therapist may most often come into question. This list below is by no means all-inclusive, but it offers an
overview of some of the possible problem areas.

Standards of Conduct Relating to:

1. competence
2. continuing education
3. confidentiality
4. duty to warn
5. sexual relationships with clients
6. dual relationships
7. informed consent
8. consultation
9. group work
10. counselor personal needs
11. termination and referral
12. inappropriate financial gain
13. research and publication
14. advertising, announcements and representations
16. complaints and violations
17. display of license
18. corporate practice
19. felony convictions

Disclosure is the practice of honestly reporting all information related to treatment in a way that insures confidentiality and promotes
open communication between all parties involved in the process. It is
usually given to the person in therapy before treatment begins.

Some therapists find it useful to draft a *Disclosure Statement,* which is
signed by the therapist and the person entering treatment (or his/her
representative) at the beginning of the therapeutic process. Many clients

may not be capable of understanding such a statement. If this is the case, a parent/guardian or advocate would act as representative to read and sign the document. An example of a disclosure statement follows.

Disclosure Statement

As you come to me for music therapy, it is my obligation to do everything in my power to help you as an individual to make progress in the areas of your life that may need improvement. I do not try to "fix" people but am usually able to assist them in "fixing" themselves.

I believe that music therapy offers many avenues of assistance not available in other therapies, because music influences human behavior in many different ways. Music therapy treats the total individual, and it provides a foundation and structure upon which new skills may be developed and existing skills enhanced.

As a music therapist, I will use music to assist you in making changes that you want to make in your life. I will work with you to plan definite goals and objectives in areas that you consider important and will assist you in measuring your success or lack of same in the areas that we address.

I will honor the ethics of my profession by maintaining strict confidentiality concerning everything that occurs in our sessions, with the exception of information that is required by law. If you feel that music therapy is not beneficial, you may discontinue this service at any time. Likewise, I will inform you if I feel that we are making no progress in our sessions.

Our signatures indicate that we have read and discussed this document together and that we agree with the principles set forth.

_____   _____
Individual Receiving Treatment   John Doe, MT-BC

It is important to understand the difference between professional disclosure and "self-expression." As a music therapist, it is seldom productive to speak about one's *innermost thoughts* regarding the treatment of an individual. To illustrate this point we offer these three scenarios:

1. You have treated many individuals with a diagnosis and behavioral traits similar to the person in treatment. The individuals treated previously did not respond well to music therapy. Based upon these experiences, your intuition tells you that perhaps the person at hand will not show good responses to your intervention. It is enough that you must wrestle with these thoughts internally; it would be irresponsible to disclose this information, for fear that you would be setting the stage for failure and allowing this information to possibly become a self-fulfilling prophecy. When you read this, you will probably think "that's just common sense," but there are persons (including therapists) who clearly do not understand the boundary between information that is productive and information that is best kept to oneself.

2. From your experience you believe that neither you nor the music that is your medium can "cure" the individual who is seeking relief. To disclose such a

thought verbally would serve no useful purpose. What you also believe is that you, with the help of the powerful medium of music, can *assist* the individual to learn new ways of dealing with stress, new ways of developing life skills, and new behaviors that may replace those that have been a causal factor in his/her distress. Everything that a therapist does in treating an individual will *communicate* thoughts and feelings, and therefore, oral explanation of this information is seldom necessary.

3. At some time during a therapeutic encounter, you may develop the *attitude* that you know the individual in treatment better than his parents, guardians, or siblings (possible countertransference). To disclose such a "feeling" would make you look extremely foolish (and rightfully so, because it is a foolish notion). Your words might only be interpreted as a message of disregard and distrust of the many hours that parents, guardians, and/or siblings have devoted to the care of the person in treatment. It is true that, as a professional music therapist, your knowledge and training provides you a unique *perspective* regarding each person that you serve, but it is the "persons in the trenches" (parents, guardians, siblings) who most often *know* the individual better than anyone else.

EXAMPLES OF ETHICAL VIOLATIONS

AMTA divides its **Code of Ethics** into twelve sections:

1. professional competence and responsibilities
2. general standards
3. relationships with clients/students/research subjects
4. relationships with colleagues
5. relationships with employers
6. responsibility to community/public
7. responsibility to the profession/association
8. research
9. fees and commercial activities
10. announcing services
11. education (teaching, supervision, administration)
12. implementation

In each of the following paragraphs, there is at least one ethical violation. Determine the violation(s) and then see if you can find the section of the **Code of Ethics** (available on-line at www.musictherapy.org or in the AMTA Sourcebook) that describes the offense. The answers for all of the examples are given at the conclusion of the last paragraph.

A. An ad appears in a local newspaper in a city in Texas that says: "Experience the inner healing and peace that come through music therapy. If you suffer from depression, anxiety, broken relationships, substance abuse, or other distressing maladies, make an appointment today with John Doe, MT-BC. Phone 444-4444." In the center of the ad is the logo of AMTA.

B. George Stringburner, MT-BC, supervises the music therapy clinic at a university in the state of New York. After he does assessments for persons who are referred to the university, he suggests that more individualized services may be found at his private "off campus" clinic. He mentions that the fees there are somewhat higher than those at the university clinic, but offers a discount if persons sign up within thirty days.

C. Mrs. Atkins has Mr. Stringburner complete a music therapy assessment for her son Jason (age 6). She mentions that Jason receives group music therapy services from Mrs. Jameson at the public school where Jason attends. When the assessment is finished, she requests services at the music therapy clinic. Without making any calls or sending any messages to Mrs. Jameson, Mr. Stringburner schedules sessions for Jason at the clinic.

D. Ginny Gleeclub, Ph.D., MT-BC, is a professor in music therapy at Cloudhook College. The students in her psychology of music class become interested in experiential music therapy. At their suggestion, Dr. Gleeclub organizes a weekly group session in which she becomes the therapist.

E. Fran Fishburger, MT-BC, is a music therapist at the Moondog Middle School in Smallville, Indiana. In conversations at home with her husband, she frequently mentions students in her sessions using their full names. She always has some good stories to tell.

F. Carl Clueless, MT-BC, is music therapist at the Smallville Developmental Center. He is a bachelor who treats all of the persons he serves with respect and dignity. In his spare time Carl spends time at Big Bob's Topless Bar, where he relaxes with his buddies. He feels that what he does on his own time is certainly his business.

G. Georgia Onmymind, an individual who lives at the Smallville Center, tells Carl that her boyfriend has been touching her in inappropriate places. Carl knows that Georgia has a reputation for making up stories about other people, so he disregards the remarks as pure fantasy.

H. George Stringburner gets a call from the local Rotary Club asking him to talk to them about music therapy on a specified day. George is really not interested in this sort of thing, so he tells them he has a schedule conflict (which is really not true). He does not refer them to a colleague who might be able to help them.

I. Jim Vandingo, Ph.D., MT-BC, is a professor of music therapy at Cloudhook College and President of AMTA. In his travels and meetings with music executives, the Yamagoochi Corporation offers him a contract to be spokesperson for their line of rhythm instruments. The contract specifies that his office with the association will never be mentioned in any advertising or promotion. Jim decides to accept the contract.

J. Joshua Jordaloon, MT-BC, wants to do research with homeless persons. After visiting several shelters, he finds that there is a lot of mistrust in the homeless community, and no one wants to participate. Joshua decides to verbally offer each participant a ten dollar bill (under the table). He soon has more subjects than he needs.

K. Cindy Crenwinkle, MT-BC, has a private practice in Stillville, Kentucky. Most of the individuals she sees pay privately, so she understands that money is generally not a problem for them. In many instances, she recommends materials (instruments, music, etc.) that will be used in treatment. She always suggests that they purchase these at the Backburner's Music House. The manager at Backburner's has a list (provided by Cindy) of persons who may be making purchases. Whenever one of these persons makes a purchase, Cindy gets a commission. Since it was her recommendation that brought them to the store, she should certainly get part of the "action."

Violations Described in the Preceding Paragraphs

A. Paragraph 1.1 in the **Code of Ethics** says that the music therapist will "perform only those duties for which he/she has been adequately trained." In the State of Texas, the "maladies" mentioned in John Doe's ad would require treatment by a Licensed Professional Counselor (LPC). Mr. Doe does not appear to have this credential. In Paragraph 10.4, the Code states that one should avoid misrepresentation of specialty, guarantees or false expectations, and the use of the Association's logo." The term "inner healing and peace" is a red flag among professional music therapists, because it sounds like the promises of medicine shows of the early 1900s that sold "magic tonic" (with a large percentage of alcohol) guaranteed to cure everything from hepatitis to "hives."

B. Paragraph 5.6 in the **Code of Ethics** states that the music therapist "will not use his/her position to obtain clients for private practice, unless authorized to do so by the employing agency." From the information given, we do not know that this is not allowed, but it is unlikely. Offering a "discount" to sign up within a certain period of time probably "discredits the profession" and "decreases the trust of the public" as stated in Paragraph 10.1. A more delicate ethical issue arises when a therapist leaves one employer and goes to another or enters private practice. It would probably be less than ethical to suggest that clients follow the therapist into a new domain; however, if the clients make decisions on their own to make this move, the question of ethics becomes *theirs* and not those of the therapist.

C. Paragraph 4.2 in the **Code of Ethics** states that the music therapist "will not offer professional services to a person receiving music therapy from another music therapist except by agreement with that therapist or after termination of the client's relationship with that therapist." One might take this to a higher level by suggesting that a therapist inquire at first meeting or contact whether the individual is receiving services from another music therapist. If the answer is "yes," then the ethical thing to do would be to contact the other therapist even before an assessment is scheduled.

D. Paragraph 3.5 in the **Code of Ethics** states that the music therapist "will not enter into dual relationships with clients/students/research subjects and will avoid those situations that interfere with professional judgment." The situation described in the example could develop quite innocently, since the professor is interested in teaching her students more about the techniques involved in experiential therapy; however, because this experience would set up the possibility of students becoming more like "patients," it is not recommended.

E. Paragraph 3.12.1 of the **Code of Ethics** states that the music therapist "protects the confidentiality of information obtained in the course of practice, supervision, teaching, and/or research." If Mrs. Fishburger used no names in discussing her clients with her husband, then, technically, no violation of confidentiality has occurred. If her husband is the kind who might go to his buddies and say, "Do you know what one of the kids at my wife's school did yesterday?", her stories could possibly be damaging to the school and/or to the children in some way. A person should know his/her spouse well enough to prevent such a scenario.

F. Paragraph 2.3.1 of the **Code of Ethics** states that the music therapist "respects the social and moral expectations of the community in which he/she works." What Carl does on his own time is his business, as long as his business is conducted behind closed doors and outside the public eye.

G. Paragraph 1.8 of the **Code of Ethics** states that the music therapist "accords sexual harassment grievants and respondents dignity and respect." This means that, in spite of the reputation of Miss Onmymind, Carl would be required by law in some states to report her claims to her social worker (or other appropriate authority) for further investigation.

H. Paragraph 6.1 of the **Code of Ethics** states that the music therapist will "strive to increase public awareness of music therapy." Getting back to the basics of the Rotary **Four Way Test** (Is it true?), the therapist told a lie when he said he had a schedule conflict. The caller did not know this, so George excused his own conduct in his own mind. Everyone (including George) would have been better served if he had said, "Presentations before service clubs are not my forte. Let me see if I can find a colleague of mine to agree to be your guest speaker."

I. Paragraph 7.4 of the **Code of Ethics** states that the music therapist "will refrain from the misuse of an official position within the association." Even though the Yamagoochi Corporation agreed to never mention Dr. Vandingo's office in the association in their advertising, the fact remains most people *know* that he has this official position, and it is probably this affiliation that formed the basis of the corporation seeking his services.

J. Paragraph 8.2 of the **Code of Ethics** states that "participation of subjects in music therapy research will be voluntary." We hear of medical studies in which the participants will receive "free medication" during the term of the research, and this is understandable since we would not expect subjects to have to pay out of their own pockets to participate. In some instances, volunteers are compensated for time away from their work, but money paid "under the table" is quite a different matter.

K. Paragraph 9.7 of the **Code of Ethics** states that the music therapist "will not profit from the sale of equipment/materials to clients." Some would say that this is unfair, since, as Ms. Crenwinkle stated, it was her recommendation that brought customers to the store. Ethics and fairness are very much alike, but ethics and *greed* do not occupy the same space at any time. Paragraph 3.12.1 of the Code states that the music therapist "protects the confidentiality of information obtained in the course of practice." For Ms. Crenwinkle to provide the manager at Backburner's with a list of names of her clientele was a clear and flagrant violation of professional ethics.

STUDY QUESTIONS FOR CHAPTER 9

1. The text lists four "pitfalls" in the practice of music therapy that lend themselves to possible ethical violations. Discuss each of these briefly.
2. **Ethics** may be defined as an a_____ that promotes actions that are not s_____, that are good for everyone concerned, that will do no h_____ to those involved, and that comply with the laws and moral codes of s_____.
3. The **Four Way Test** from *Rotary International* offers a good basic set of guidelines for ethical behavior.
   1. Is it the t_____?
   2. Is it f_____ to all concerned?
   3. Will it build g_____ will and better friendships?
   4. Will it be b_____ to all concerned?
4. The AMTA **Code of Ethics** covers the profession and the practice. What does the CBMT **Code of Professional Practice** cover?
5. **Disclosure** is the practice of h_____ reporting all information related to treatment in a way that insures c_____ and

promotes open c_____ between all parties involved in the process.

6. In the *Disclosure Statement* that is included in this chapter, several important considerations are mentioned. Answer the questions below:
    (a) Is the therapist promising to "fix" or "heal" the individual seeking treatment?
    (b) What claims does the therapist make for music therapy?
    (c) Why do you suppose goals and objectives are mentioned?
    (d) Is *all* information regarding the therapist-client relationship always confidential?
    (e) Who decides when music therapy is no longer helpful to an individual?

7. What is the difference between **disclosure** and "self-expression"?

8. Why is the "intuition" of the therapist regarding treatment of an individual usually best kept to himself/herself?

9. If you believe that neither you nor the medium of music can "heal" an individual, why would you not just state this position "up front"?

10. Describe a situation in which a music therapist might have a very good reason for feeling that he/she knows more about the person in treatment than the individual's parents, guardians, or siblings.

Chapter 10

AN INTRODUCTION TO RESEARCH

- Preliminary Considerations
- Research Defined
- Different Types of Research
- What is NOT Research?
- Practical Applications of Your Skills

PRELIMINARY CONSIDERATIONS

Many music therapists seem to have difficulty establishing a connection between research and their everyday practice. As mentioned in Chapter 1, the development of a significant research base is one of the key factors in promoting acceptance of the field of music therapy as a legitimate part of the health professions in general. In Chapter 2 there was reference to the importance of the **scientific approach**, that is, basing our practice upon research to provide a rational theory for what we do.

It is our opinion that students and other interested persons should begin their introduction to research in music therapy by learning to locate, read, and evaluate the literature with some degree of understanding. Articles that are available provide information about persons at all levels of life skills development, strategies that relate to music therapy, all of the various conditions mentioned in this text, and music therapy practices in various clinical settings.

RESEARCH DEFINED

When we look up a telephone number, it is a *search* for information that is *established* as fact. *Research* implies a quest that goes beyond that which is established. If we separate the word into its component parts, the prefix *re* means "again," and active verb *search* means "to seek." Research, therefore, means that we are taking a second or perhaps closer look at phenomena that are already apparent in hopes of gaining new understanding or discovering new frontiers of information.

Scientific research implies the use of specific principles and guidelines related to the *scientific method*. These include objectivity of observations within an accepted structure, some form of measurement of phenomena, and the formulation and testing of a *hypothesis*. The meaning of the word *hypothesis* becomes clearer when we apply the same principle of separation of its component parts. A *thesis* is an "idea," and the prefix *hypo* means "below"; therefore, a *hypothesis* is a statement which, if proven through research may become a *thesis* (or theory).

Some understanding of the special language of scientific research may help the beginner read studies more easily. The term *significance* is often misunderstood. Because of the common use of this word, one might assume that what is "significant" is also "important." This is not always the case. In research, the word *significant* refers specifically to the statistical probability that the results occurred beyond chance (50–50) at a certain level or probability (.01 or .05). If "significance" is listed as .05, it means that the results occurred beyond chance with the probability of 95 out of 100 trials. If it is listed as .01, the probability of results having occurred beyond chance is even greater (99 of 100 trials). Even if the results do not meet these accepted levels of significance, information contained in the studies may still be important to the field of music therapy. If the data are from a "pilot" study (investigating new phenomena), the importance of the information may be enhanced.

DIFFERENT TYPES OF RESEARCH

As in the case of any type of observation, *research* may be further categorized as *quantitative* or *qualitative*. Research that tests hypotheses and documents responses in numerical values may be called *quantitative*. Research that may ultimately generate experimental hypotheses but relies upon subjective data is usually called *qualitative*.

To say that a study is *qualitative* does *not* mean that it is simply a narrative of someone's observations. Many aspects of a *qualitative* study may be converted to *quantitative* data, e.g., if a videotape record of procedures is analyzed for relevant numerical measurements.

Qualitative observation of early developmental behaviors may be quantified by using the Music Therapy Assessment Profile (MTAP: Michel & Rohrbacher, 1983). A videotape of an assessment of a ten-year-old girl with a diagnosis of autism was presented to a college class, who watched it and marked MTAP data forms where specific behaviors indicated functional developmental skill levels. The class agreed 100 percent in concluding that the child for the most part exhibited behaviors at a developmental level of two and one half years. Ultimately, such information could be used as a baseline for music therapy intervention (Pinson & Michel, 1999).

Experimental research is a way of testing an idea or *hypothesis* under controlled conditions. These controls may include a comparison between experimental groups and control groups and/or a comparison of experimental conditions with a single group. Research of this type yields statistical information, which may provide direction for future investigation.

Research that is not *experimental* is sometimes referred to as *descriptive*. Surveys, focus groups, historical, and other types of research are sometimes in this category. Hypotheses are possible in descriptive research in terms of predicted *correlational values*, but here one must always remember that high correlations of two variables, such as smoking and lung cancer, do not necessarily mean causation. To remember this, one can say, "correlations only indicate relationships–not causation!"

Survey research is considered to be scientific and is usually *quantitative* (observing what is) but not necessarily *experimental* (manipulating variables). Since data from surveys are *quantitative*, they sometimes produce correlations between different observed factors that may be used for statistical predictions. For example, when a voter survey predicts outcomes of an election, it is reported to be within certain "margins of error," which is determined from formulas developed for such data. Prediction from survey data must be done with care, but even if done carefully, the results can sometimes be very misleading–as shown in the wrong predictions of the outcome of the 2000 presidential election in the USA.

Marketing researchers develop focus groups in which people are asked to respond to a series of questions about a product or service. From this information may come ideas for follow-up with quantitative studies, such as surveys of larger groups of subjects. An example in the health field is a study by Davis et al. (2002) in which a group of elderly persons were asked to discuss problems with barriers they experienced in seeking relief from pain. Their responses were tabulated (qualitative into quantitative), and the resulting data were analyzed to generate hypotheses for future studies.

Historical research is another important type of research that is similar to a survey. This is often done as a preliminary part of other types of research (as noted earlier), reviewing studies that have been done in the past. It is also a legitimate part of research about which it is often said, "If we do not learn from the past, we may suffer repeating the errors of the past." In this type of research, an important part is identifying where to find historic materials.

One of the sources of such data is in archives, usually found in libraries. They preserve materials from the past and are very important in specific fields of study. The American Music Therapy Association National Archives is located at the Colorado State University in Fort Collins. Several of the AMTA regions also maintain their own archives, e.g., archives of the Southwestern Region of AMTA are located at the Texas Woman's University Library in Denton.

Current technology not only allows for audio and visual recordings and actual programs, but also provides easier access to such materials through the internet (see Appendix).

WHAT IS *NOT* RESEARCH?

As stated previously, scientific research implies the criteria of *objectivity*. Some reports of individual cases ("anecdotal" stories about the benefits of music therapy) should not be labeled "research"; however, there are statistical measures that may be applied to "single case studies" that make them more objective and predictable for replication. In this text, case examples usually reflect underlying principles derived from scientific research.

Within the "non-research" category of music therapy literature, one finds many examples of "pseudo-research" or that which is claimed to be research but does not meet scientific requirements. One reference for this type of research is found in Summer's book, *Music, the New Age Elixir* (1996), which critically examines studies that claim mystical or magical results but which are not objective or supported by scientific research. AMTA has a Professional Advocacy Committee for monitoring and investigating questionable publications and practices in and around the field of music therapy.

In reading case studies or actual research, one must be very skeptical of gross "generalities" made by persons whose sole aim is to make the most of anything startling or "newsworthy." If the claims made by such persons seem a bit unrealistic or "overblown," one should request the published results or a copy of the original research from which the generalities were derived. This is not to say that case studies are not of some value when used as examples, as in this text; however, they should not be called "scientific research."

PRACTICAL APPLICATION OF YOUR SKILLS

The process of reading research with understanding is a skill that develops gradually as you learn more about the field and as you experience first hand the effects of the music therapy process. There is a lot of information available, but you must learn to screen the offerings to determine what is useful to you as an individual. Below is an outline that will help to guide you in your initial exploration of the many offerings in professional journals, masters degree theses, doctoral dissertations, and books on the subject of music therapy.

1 **Read the *abstract* at the beginning, if this is part of the document.**
   An *abstract* is a condensed summary of the research that provides an introduction and an overview of the procedures used and the information gathered. It may serve as a screening device to determine the value of the research in terms of your present needs.

2. **Skip to the *discussion* at the end of the document.**
   The *discussion* contains a conclusion, which will usually summarize the results of the study and, in some instances, make recommendations regarding possible applications of the research and/or needs for further exploration.

3. **Determine the *purpose* of the research.**
   As you read the *discussion,* look for the stated or unstated *purpose* of the study. If it is unstated or difficult to understand, express it in your own words.

4. **Determine the *results* of the study. Were any conclusions drawn from these results?**
   A recent study (Brotons & Kroger, 2000) demonstrated that in patients diagnosed with Dementia of the Alzheimer's Type (DAT), speech content and fluency were better following music therapy

(experimental condition) when compared to strictly "conversational" sessions with a therapist (controlled condition). The report of this comparison is the *results*. The authors further stated that "music therapy interventions may positively influence the speech content and fluency in people affected by DAT." This statement forms the conclusion, which in this case is just a more general statement of the results.

5. **Evaluate the importance of this information with regard to music therapy in general and to your own experiences.**
   If you have observed persons with dementia, or if you have a family member who is diagnosed in this way, this information will lend new credibility to the use of music therapy with such persons.

How can we know whether or not a research study is valid? One way to assess validity is to find related articles in the same area and, if possible, a critical review of the research. Most professional journals in the medical and health areas provide critiques from other research scholars on new studies in their fields. Sometimes original research is seriously questioned about procedures that tend to diminish the validity of the study. Professional journals often encourage the original researcher to respond to such criticism, and the dialogue that may ensue can be very healthy for all concerned.

One other factor in scientific research that is sometimes overlooked is replicability. This refers to whether or not enough details are provided to produce a similar study relative to procedures and materials used. One could not anticipate similar results without having sufficient details. In some music therapy studies, there is lack of information regarding specific music used and how it was used. Music therapists sometimes categorize music as sedative, stimulative, etc. and fail to understand the importance of more complete descriptions, especially when reporting the results of research (Michel & Chesky, 1996).

Research studies have been cited throughout this book. More information may be found in the Appendix, which contains resources that are available on the internet.

STUDY QUESTIONS FOR CHAPTER 10

1. The development of a significant research base is one of the key factors in promoting _____ of the field of music therapy.
2. Define the word *research*.

3. A *thesis* is the statement of an idea. What is a *hypotheses?*
4. The word *significant* refers specifically to the statistical probability that the results occurred beyond _____ (50–50) at a certain level or _____ (.01 or .05).

5. **RESEARCH THAT TESTS HYPOTHESES RELATIVE TO THE PRACTICE OF MUSIC THERAPY AND DOCUMENTS RESPONSES IN NUMERICAL VALUES MAY BE CALLED _____.**

6. Research that may ultimately generate experimental hypotheses but relies upon subjective data is usually called _____.
7. *Experimental research* is a way of testing something (an idea or *hypothesis*) under _____ conditions.
8. Survey research is considered to be scientific and is usually _____ (observing what is) but not necessarily _____ (manipulating variables).
9. What is an *abstract?*
10. What is the purpose of the *discussion* in an article reporting research?
11. If "significance" in a study is listed as .05, what does that mean?
12. Does a study whose results do not meet accepted levels of significance have any importance to the field of music therapy?
13. Importance of the information reported may be enhanced if the data are from a "_____" study (investigating new phenomena).
14. Is it ever possible to convert the results of a *qualitative* study into *quantitative* data? What type of technology available in most settings would make this possibility more likely?
15. In reading case studies or actual research, one must be very skeptical of "gross" "_____" made by persons whose sole aim is to make the most of anything startling or "newsworthy."

Chapter 11

LOOKING BACK–LOOKING AHEAD

- Summary
- Visions of the Future (Michel)
- And Furthermore (Pinson)
- Concluding Remarks

SUMMARY

This book is intended as a direct and simplified approach to the field of music therapy. It speaks to the beginning student as well as to his/her parents and others who are perhaps unfamiliar with but interested in the practice of music therapy. We have approached our specialty from the standpoint of Principles and Practices in order to introduce music therapy as an active member of the health professions. We have presented what we believe to be reliable and relevant information about music therapy as a profession with over fifty years of research and reported practices in professional journals, including those in our own field: *The Journal of Music Therapy and Music Therapy Perspectives.*

To describe the field and to increase understanding in more specific ways, we have presented a theory/model of music therapy, the Michel **Stress and Developmental Skills Model,** and have used examples of practice that include firsthand accounts of clinical experiences of each of the authors. Many of these examples are supported by research.

Accountability issues in music therapy, such as the use of appropriate assessment tools by professional music therapists, have been addressed under the area of practical applications and also as they relate to ethical issues. Models of disclosure appropriate for music therapists have been provided. Clinical and educational settings in which music therapists

130

now practice have been described, as well as the wide range of individual practice and research that is evident around the world.

An introduction to research, especially as it applies to music therapy, is included. Attention is called to the need for music therapists to be constantly aware of research as it may apply to their clinical practice as well as its importance in extending the field through applications in medical and rehabilitation settings.

Attention has also been directed to "What is NOT research" in music therapy. This includes encouraging awareness of misrepresentations found in many publications today and calling attention to them. This is to alert future professional music therapists to be aware of "mystical" or "magical" claims of therapeutic values and "new" types of music therapy that are unsubstantiated by scientific research; however, we also recognize that there are reasons to accept the conclusions of experienced professional music therapists whose work has been proven effective but which may not have been supported by formal research. Many of the case studies in this book are based upon established principles, but the application in specific settings and with specific populations has not always been the subject of controlled studies. One of the exciting aspects of our field is the fact that many areas of practice have not been fully explored with the scientific method, and this represents a significant challenge for those who are preparing for a career in music therapy.

Finally, we present here some ideas about the possible future of music therapy as a profession based upon our observations of current trends in the field and our personal ideas about where we would like to see progressive development.

VISIONS OF THE FUTURE (MICHEL)

In *Music Therapy Perspectives,* a review of the history of the profession comparing the original goals of the national organization to the current developments and some ideas of what the future might hold for music therapists were presented (Michel, 2000). The author emphasized the importance of the professional organization (formerly the National Association for Music Therapy, now the American Music Therapy Association) and how its policies could influence the future of the field. Areas of influence included the association's emphasis on some of the original goals such as informing the public about music therapy (public relations and/or publicity), setting educational and clinical standards for the field, continuing research, gaining acceptance of facilitating organizations (medical associations and health care providers), and identifying funding sources (private foundations, private insurance and the resources of federal and state governments).

Professional music therapists (most Music Therapists-Board Certified and some using the credential Registered Music Therapist) are working in many different clinical and educational settings and under a variety of working conditions which include salaried positions, part-time salaried or contract positions, and private contract or fee work. A survey conducted in 2001 indicated that music therapists were working with the following populations: elderly and Alzheimers, developmentally disabled, neurological, medical and surgical, and a wide variety of forty-four other populations and settings (AMTA 2003).

The total number of professional music therapists in the world is relatively small when compared with persons working in the areas of speech, physical, and occupational therapy. This disparity is sometimes difficult to understand. Perhaps the best, but not the only factor is that music therapy is not listed in most guidelines and regulations for professional services required in clinical settings. These guidelines are the key to funding and the creation of more positions for music therapists.

I recommend that more connections be made with advisors from medical and health care fields to explore ways of gaining further recognition in the established guidelines. A group of retired music therapists and educators has recommended that AMTA seek an outside evaluation of the field to determine changes needed to improve the association for the purpose of gaining the status that we deserve.

In the future, these recommendations may lead to even more recognition and acceptance of music therapy by the health-care and medical professions as well as by the general public. Demand for professional music therapists will be greater and similar to that for other therapists. The field for applications of music therapy will be expanding, e.g., wellness programs, hospice, and interventions in general medical settings.

The unique contributions of music therapy will be better understood by potential employers, not just as a collaborative therapy but also as a primary one of choice. Future employers will understand the potentially powerful use of music as a tool used by professional music therapists, and that music therapy training is different from that of performers and educators. They will also understand that there are no easy "formulas" for selection of music used in therapy, i.e., that there is a wide variety of choices beyond what the therapist and person in treatment may "like." Professional music therapists understand that the choice of music is usually based upon research and knowledge of the functional aspects of the medium–not just the styles or types of music that we generally associate with certain individuals or groups.

Future employers will also understand that music therapy can be applied throughout a wide variety of diseases, disorders, and disabilities as well as in the improvement or establishment of most of the life-span developmental skills needed for specific individuals. Techniques and protocols employed by music therapists will follow, and often lead, new developments in different health fields, e.g., working with the neurology of the human brain and peripheral neural systems in such areas as pain management and stroke rehabilitation, following pioneering work done by earlier researchers such as Chesky and Michel (1996) and Thaut (2000).

In the field of health care (medical interventions), more extensive research will be done in the area of brain functioning, and studies will follow medical models, i.e., using placebo, double blind, and clinical trials methods. Some persons (Chesky, Michel, Thaut, Tims) are already involved in this type of research, and there appears to be a growing demand for this kind of data.

In the area of life skills (special education or alternate education), researchers follow different models, i.e., behavioral (not anecdotal) and studies that are qualitative as well as quantitative in design. Research of this type paves the way for establishing protocols regarding priorities in skill development, and allows therapists to fine tune the techniques used in these types of intervention.

Health areas such as wellness, or preventative medicine, are in wide acceptance and use. Music therapists are practicing in these areas, which in the past, followed the psychological definition of "Subjective Well Being" that included many areas of human behavior familiar to music therapy practice:

1. Assisting persons in controlling moods (positive and negative)
2. Assisting persons with the development of personality
3. Assisting persons who need to learn work skills that offer stimulation and positive social interaction
4. Assisting persons who need to improve social skills during leisure time by participation in an organized music ensembles

5. Assisting persons in developing performance opportunities that can increase self-esteem and self-efficacy (Michel & Martin, 1970, Michel & Farrell, 1973).

The challenge for educators will be to keep abreast of the latest information in music therapy and to present it to future students in a way that they can learn and internalize these concepts. In music therapy, some of the greatest breakthroughs in learning occur when the student *applies* the techniques learned in class in his/her practicum experiences. The reality and unpredictable nature of the moment provides a realistic framework for making the information and skills *relevant* to the needs of the student and the particular population being served.

AND FURTHERMORE (PINSON)

Professional music therapists in the future will be better prepared in their "functional" music skills. Some of our music colleagues have some problems with that term "functional"–saying that certainly one needs to have music skills that are *more* than that. If they mean that we should become concert artists, I would remind them that many pianists with well-developed "chops" for recreating and interpreting the works of the great masters can't play *Happy Birthday* without a sheet of music in front of them. Likewise, many gifted flautists, clarinetists, etc. who do extremely well with solos that they have memorized would be *totally* lost in a jazz ensemble. Developing skills in performance does not necessarily include the kind of abilities that we need. "Functional" is defined as a *healthy* balance of the following skills:

a. the ability to improvise a keyboard or guitar accompaniment for most standard songs–preferably in more than one key
b. the ability to lead singing in a manner that inspires confidence and participation (at some level) on the part of persons in treatment
c. the ability to adapt most standard lead sheets and basic print music on the keyboard and guitar to provide a structure for participation
d. the ability to transpose single line notation for any instrument of the band or orchestra
e. the ability to compose and arrange music for solo or an ensemble that provides each participant with a successful experience

f. the ability to access and utilize current and developing technology in the creation of music therapy strategies

The list above seems to be more than any student could possibly develop during the average four-year academic program, and it represents a significant challenge to educators to provide the knowledge and experience necessary to accomplish these objectives. New concepts about music theory, especially as it relates to chord motion, are being developed and already in use in some academic programs (Pinson, 2000). Thanks to the technology that is available, students have immediate access to sounds and styles of music that would at one time have required a lifetime of experience.

Professional music therapists in the future will find greater acceptance of their work and of the persons whom they serve. The great gulf of misunderstanding that has always existed between the "normals" and those who don't quite measure up to that term is getting smaller, because there is greater awareness (and possibly greater acceptance) of persons with disabilities. Where the distance from shore to shore is still significant, it should be the obligation of the professional music therapist to assist in building bridges of understanding. This can be done in many ways, but here are a few suggestions:

a. by assisting music educators with integrating special learners into their performing groups
b. by assisting special educators with music strategies that enhance learning and take advantage of unique individual abilities
c. by presenting general information about music therapy that includes success stories to civic groups in your area
d. by developing performing ensembles of persons with disabilities and finding audiences who can embrace their music making
e. by arranging and adapting music for joint performance by persons with special needs (individuals or ensembles) and community choirs, bands, etc.
f. by supporting our national organization with its efforts to define and refine the techniques that are most successful in developing the unique talents of persons with disabilities

Professional music therapists in the future will be more "connected" with the medical establishment, because studies and research will continue to validate the positive effects of music on the various systems of the body and its influence on general well-being. Those in our profession can assist this process in the following ways:

    a. by networking with physicians and persons in other therapeutic disciplines to share ideas and cultivate friendships based upon our common interest in the well-being of those we serve

    b. by using the medium of music in your own life to keep your mind occupied, to stimulate your creativity, to fine tune your functional skills, and as a vehicle for sharing your good fortune with others

    c. by encouraging our national organization to develop more specific and dynamic affiliations with the medical community and other professional therapists

    d. by being an *active* listener who understands that musical expression is usually "from the heart" and, therefore, a key to understanding all people.

CONCLUDING REMARKS

A person in a music therapy group once made the observation, "Music therapy is kind of a *sneaky* therapy." When asked what that meant, he explained that it is so much fun, that the therapy kind of sneaks up on you without your knowing it. Participation in making music is generally fun for most people. Even though working on the rudiments may involve concentration and some practice, the end result is usually very satisfying.

The same cannot be said for many of the other therapeutic disciplines. Some of them have incorporated music in their regimens with some success, but this is usually recorded selections that fall short of the more intense musical involvement that may be provided by a professional music therapist. Occupational therapy, physical therapy, and medical interventions usually involve a lot of necessary touching and/or manipulation of limbs. For persons who are physically challenged, it may be a "breath of fresh air" to encounter a therapist whose major mode does not require physical contact. In a very real sense, music therapy has the ability to touch without touching.

Compared to other therapeutic disciplines, music therapy is generally very cost effective. At least three reasons can account for this: (1) Music therapy may be done effectively in small groups–thus reducing the per-person fee. (2) A good part of what is done in music therapy is similar to music lessons that usually involve homework and practice. (3) The music itself contains elements that are generally positive and motivating. If a person in treatment gets involved in these aspects of the process, the effectiveness of the therapy is usually enhanced.

For the future music therapist, the profession promises the same potential "sneaky" rewards that are enjoyed by the clientele. If you are having fun doing the things that your profession requires, you are probably on the right track. The world of "inner space" (how people learn, how they react, how they behave) probably has more unknowns than the explorations to other planets; therefore, the music therapist who incorporates research in his/her practice experiences the natural high of discovering new principles and ideas that are beneficial to other persons. The gift of music in a therapeutic context is, more than anything, a gift of one's self to another person–offered without the expectation of anything in return. Regardless of your compensation (or lack of same), this principle remains as one of the finer elements of our profession.

APPENDIX

INTERESTING WEB SITES

At the time this list of web sites was drafted, these were all working and in good order. The nature of the internet is fluctuating; therefore, it is possible that some of these are no longer working.

www.aboutproduce.com–This site is for persons considering the vegetarian life.

www.accordionheaven.com–Source for accordions (new and used), instruction, and technical support.

www.adaa.org–Site of the Anxiety Disorders Association of America, which offers resources for clinicians, researchers and other treatment providers in all disciplines.

www.adaptivation.com–Adaptivation designs, manufactures and distributes assistive technology to persons with disabilities.

www.adta.org–The American Dance Therapy Association promotes high standards in the field of dance/movement therapy.

www.advancedbrain.com–Advanced Brain Technologies is the creator of innovative brain-based products and technologies for therapeutic, educational, and self-improvement benefits.

www.allkindsofminds.org–All Kinds of Minds provides programs, tools, and a common language for parents, educators, and clinicians to help students with differences in learning achieve success in the classroom and in life.

www.alz.org–Site of The Alzheimer's Association, the largest national voluntary health organization supporting Alzheimer's research and care.

www.ambucs.com–AMBUCS is an organization dedicated to creating opportunities for independence for people with disabilities. They also provide scholarships for therapists.

www.americaslibrary.com–This site, produced by the Library of Congress, gives historical information and also words and music to a lot of songs.

www.aosa.org–Site of the American Orff Schulwerk Association.

www.apa.org–Site of the American Psychological Association. Late breaking news, journal information, and related links.

www.aspergerinfo.com–Site developed by the parents of a child with Asperger's syndrome to provide information to other parents.

www.athealth.com–A leading provider of mental health information and services for mental health practitioners and those they serve.

139

www.atozteacherstuff.com–This site was designed to help teachers (K–12) find online lesson plans and resources more quickly and easily.

www.autismarts.com–Site of the McMurray A.R.T.S. Center and Autism Arts is to offer an open window of opportunities for our children, one in which their light can shine through to a broader community.

www.babybumblebee.com–Devoted to providing parents with educationally appropriate materials for infants and toddlers.

www.babyeinstein.com–Site that promotes the idea of exposing very young children to the greatest forms of human expression–language, poetry, art and music–in a way that they love.

www.bandofangels.com–Band of Angels Press produces printed materials (calendars, books, etc.) that celebrate the positive aspects of persons with Down syndrome.

www.barefootbooks.com–Site of Barefoot Books which markets books that inspire the imagination of children.

www.benefitscheckup.org–BenefitsCheck*Up* is a free, easy-to-use service that identifies federal and state assistance programs for older Americans.

www.bowbooks.com–BOW Books is a publisher and creator of books, audio books, and ancillary products that demonstrate values, integrity, and principles for children, parents, and significant others.

www.brainconnection.com–This site is dedicated to providing accessible, high-quality information about how the brain works and how people learn.

www.bravekids.org–Help for children with chronic, life-threatening illnesses or disabilities–a great resource directory of organizations message boards and a lot of useful information.

www.bymyside.com–This site is devoted to information about cancer treatment and support networks.

www.byregion.net–Network of Healing Arts and Artists, with primary focus on visual artists, crafters, musicians, and performing artists. Includes topics like "sound healing" and "medical music."

www.cec.sped.org–The Council for Exceptional Children (CEC) is dedicated to improving educational outcomes for individuals with exceptionalities, students with disabilities, and/or the gifted.

www.civitan.org–Web site of this civic organization whose work is dedicated to serving individual and community needs with an emphasis on helping people with developmental disabilities.

www.clas.uiuc.edu–This site provides much information regarding the use of various languages (including sign).

www.clinicaltrials.gov–A great database of experimental trials. Contains the latest new ideas for disease treatments.

www.cnsfoundation.org–Children's Neurobiological Solutions Foundation, CNS, provides information about the emerging fields of neural plasticity and repair, in hopes of securing a future filled with possibilities for our present and future children.

www.constplay.com–Constructive Playthings is a supplier of early childhood educational toys, equipment, books, records, tapes, videos, art supplies, and teaching aids.

www.creativedance.org–Creative Dance Center provides quality dance education for people of all ages.

www.customcpu.com/personal/pir/songs.htm–This site is a good source of lyrics for patriotic songs. There are also midi files available.

www.devdelay.org–Organization dedicated to meeting the needs of children who have developmental delays in sensory motor, language, social, and emotional areas.

www.difflearn.com–This site offers materials designed to help in teaching persons with autism and other developmental disabilities.

www.digipharm.com–Micro Music Laboratories®, have established a new branch of medicine and created a completely new business–Digital Pharmacy®, which has digital pharmaceutical products (CD's that may be used to treat everything from heart disease to herpes). Don't believe everything that you see here.

www.disabilityresources.org–Disability resources collects and disseminates information about legal rights, financial resources, assistive technology, employment opportunities, housing modifications, childrearing and educational options, transportation and mobility services, and more.

www.do2learn.com–This site contains activities and resources to encourage independence among persons with special learning needs.

www.docs.com–This site provides some information about electronic documentation, including SOAPware, an Electronic Medical Record designed for clinics.

www.donjohnston.com–Site offers reading, writing, word-study and computer access products, as well as services for educating teachers on using technology in the classroom to teach reading and writing.

www.drhuggiebear.com–This site contains some medical and practical advice about interventions that are useful with persons with attention deficit disorder.

www.drugdigest.org/DD/Home–This site gives information about the use and effects of many drugs used with persons with disabilities.

www.earlychildhood.com–This site offers monthly themes with related materials and activities for early childhood education.

www.easter-seals.org–Easter Seals helps individuals with disabilities and special needs, and their families.

www.eldersong.com–This site is a good source of creative activity materials for older adults.

www.fape.org–This is the site of Friends and Partners in Education, which discusses the system of special education from various standpoints.

www.fda.gov–Official site of the Food and Drug Administration.

www.fetaweb.com–At this site you will find articles, checklists, sample letters, charts and resources to supplement the book entitled *From Emotions to Advocacy* by Pam and Pete Wright.

www.50states.com–This site gives information about all of the states (capital, state song, flower, bird, etc.).

www.giraffe.org–The nonprofit Giraffe Heroes Project promotes citizenship by telling the stories of these "Giraffes" in the media, on podiums and in the K–12 Giraffe Heroes Program for schools.

www.goodgrief.org–Website of the Shiva Foundation, which offers resources and support in the grieving process. These programs are offered to individuals, families, and communities.

www.greattalkingbox.com–Company dedicated to providing all persons with any disability everything they need to make their lives as full and as complete as possible. They manufacture dependable, durable and affordable speech devices.

www.handle.org–The Handle Institute is a non-profit institute providing a non-drub alternative for identifying and treating neurodevelopmental disorders.

www.harmonycentral.com–A comprehensive site for guitarists that offers instruction and a lot of information about the instrument.

www.harpdepot.com–Website devoted entirely to harmonicas, which are sometimes called "harps" (sales, service, instruction, etc.).

www.headsupnow.com–A family website that offers practical help and encouragement to others who regularly interact with children with learning differences.

www.healthdiary.com–Health Diary looks at medical issues from the patient's point of view. Experience the personal stories that will help you take better care of your health.

www.healthjourneys.com–Image Paths, Inc., the company that produces the Health Journeys, sells guided imagery tapes, CD's, and books that enhance wellness, personal growth and healing.

www.healthwindows.com–This site is a members-only internet-based health and wellness resource.

www.herbalgram.org–Site developed by the American Botanical Council. Excellent list of books offered for purchase.

www.hotbraile.com–Site of the leading provider of web-based communication tools for the visually impaired, their friends, and family. Here you can send Braille letters, learn the Braille alphabet, meet new people, and connect with over 13,000 other HotBraille members.

www.ideapractices.org–This site provides information about with the Individuals with Disabilities Education Act (IDEA). The purpose is to inform professionals, families, and the public about strategies to improve educational results for children.

www.images.google.com–This site has images for almost any purpose. A very good resource.

www.intelihealth.com–Site developed by the Harvard Medical School. Contains easy-to-understand explanation of various diseases.

www.interactivemetronome.com–Tells about acoustical technology based on the traditional music metronome, which has been used to improve motor skills and attention to task. The

www.isme.org–Website of the International Society for Music Education.

www.janbrett.com–This site features coloring pages and art activities for children.

www.jimgill.com–Jim Gill has a master's degree in child development. He writes and performs his own songs aimed at giving children and adults a joyful music making experience. Site contains sound samples and list of CD's.

www.kentuckiana.org–Kentuckiana Children's Center has operated as an outpatient clinic, providing evaluation, treatment, and a special education program for children with special needs.

www.kidaccess.com–Website created by Jill Fain Lehman, Ph.D., who designs excellent visual icons for use with persons with communication disorders.

www.kidscontracts.com–This site provides suggestions to parents about developing contracts with their children to control behavior and to mold their abilities.

www.lillianvernon.com–This site contains a variety of colorful toys, furniture, and accessories for children and adults.

www.lonestarlearning.com–This site provides special materials for teachers (especially in the area of mathematics).

www.lorman.com–Lorman Education Services is a leading provider of continuing education seminars in the U. S. and Canada.

www.loveandlearning.com–Website focusing on ways to teach reading and language.

www.menc.org–MENC: National Association for Music Education (formerly Music Educators National Conference) promotes music education by encouraging the study and making of music by all.

www.mayoclinic.com–Thousands of the clinic's doctors from around the country contribute. It is a rich source of articles by internationally known experts.

www.medline.plus.gov–Website that contains information organized by topic. Dictionaries and encyclopedias are available.

www.millermethod.org–Web site for the The Language and Cognitive Development Center (LCDC), an internationally known, accredited nonprofit school, clinic, and training facility for the treatment of pervasively disordered (PDD) children.

www.monarchschool.org–The Monarch School is dedicated to providing a therapeutic learning environment where active minds are challenged, all are treated with respect and dignity, learning is a joy, and wisdom is the outcome.

www.mtna.org–Music Teachers National Association is a nonprofit organization of 24,000 independent and collegiate music teachers committed to furthering the art of music through programs that encourage and support teaching, performance, composition, and scholarly research.

www.music-outreach.com–Music Outreach describes the activities and recordings of Michael Purvis, who has a lot of experience performing for seniors.

www.musicminusone.com–This site offers recorded accompaniments for all instruments and vocalists.

www.musictherapy.org–official site of the American Music Therapy Association.

www.mylittlesteps.com–This site features a unique, thorough, assessment and teaching program, available on line, giving support for parents to help in their child's development and education.

www.my.webmd.com–Website containing articles about medical issues reviewed by a staff of full-time, board certified physicians.

www.ncptsd.org–The National Center for Post-Traumatic Stress Disorder (PTSD) addresses the needs of veterans with military-related PTSD.

www.ndmda.org–Web address for the Depression and Bipolar Support Alliance (DBSA), the nation's largest patient-directed, illness-specific organization.

www.NeedyMeds.com–This site is designed to provide information about patient assistance programs which provide no cost prescription medications to eligible participants.

www.neurosmith.com—Website of organization devoted to creating learning toys for children.

www.newhorizons.org—An international network of people, programs, and products dedicated to successful, innovative learning.

www.nih.gov—Site of the 27 institutes and centers that consitute the National Institutes of Health. Check out the National Center for Complementary and Alternative Medicine.

www.nimh.nih.gov—Website of the National Institute of Mental Health.

www.nmha.org—The National Mental Health Association is the country's oldest and largest nonprofit organization addressing all aspects of mental health and mental illness.

www.nsd.on.ca—This website describes an organization that trains guide dogs for persons with epilepsy, autism, etc.

www.ntxsuzukimusic.org—This is the site of the regional Suzuki organization—with information about instruction, programs, etc.

www.nutrition.gov—A doorway to over 100 health-related web pages hosted by various federal agencies.

www.partymasks.com—Website devoted to the sale of imported party masks from England, party favors, and supplies that are unique and fun.

www.pdinfo.com—This very useful site lists over 3000 songs that are in the public domain (no longer protected by copyright laws).

www.pfot.com—Pocket Full Of Therapy provides materials to assist those concerned with the development of children.

www.poetrypals.com—This site provides a safe, reality-based environment in which teachers and parents can share basic principles of learning with children.

www.preschoolprintables.com—This site is a resource for printed materials (calendars, certificates, etc.) that are useful with children.

www.proedinc.com—PRO-ED, Inc. is a leading publisher of nationally standardized tests for speech, language, hearing, psychology, counseling, special education, and rehabilitation.

www.psych.org—official site of the American Psychiatric Association.

www.psycheducation.org—This site is a resource for various psychological problems. Its long-term goal is to provide quality education on topics where information is scattered or non-existent.

www.ravennaventures.com—This site offers ideas and music related to the development of creative dance expressions.

www.reachingpotentials.org—Reaching Potentials, Inc. is a private, non-profit organization dedicated to serving the needs of individuals with autism and their families.

www.samueljohnson.com—This site provides access to over 1000 quotes from Samuel Johnson, the second most quoted person in the English language, after Shakespeare. *Ethics* is a frequent topic.

www.savantacademy.org—This organization specializes in helping blind musical savants and those Optic Nerve Hypoplasia (ONH).

www.sensoryresources.com—This site provides information about sensory integration and sensory processing.

www.shakeandlearn.com–Shake and Learn™ is a concept that utilizes creative methods that enable students to retain basic academic concepts and skills.

www.smallworldtoys.com–This site features toys that are appropriate for children with special needs.

www.songs-that-teach.com–Songs That Teach program offers all students an integrated language arts music and dictation program.

www.sound-remedies.com–Sound Remedies produces recorded music which music "people can use to improve their lives."

www.specialneedsinfo.net–This site provides information related to education, resources, supports and services available for children with disabilities and their families.

www.specialolympics.org–Special Olympics is dedicated to helping persons with mental retardation to become respected members of society through sports training and competition.

www.speechville.com–Organization dedicated to providing knowledge about available resources to help your children who have a communication impairment or disorder.

www.superduperinc.com–Source for clever, colorful, high quality materials for speech-language pathologists, special educators, teachers, parents, and caregivers in educational, home, and health care settings.

www.tabledit.com–TablEdit is a program for creating, editing, printing, and listening to tablature and sheet music (standard notation) for guitar and other fretted, stringed instruments.

www.teacherdiscoveries.com–This site has materials for the classroom teacher or the music therapist (principally elementary).

www.tendercare4kids.com–Site dedicated to providing families with access to the many unique products that caring for a child with special needs can require.

www.theideabox.com–This site contains ideas for early childhood educational resources and links to other similar sites.

www.ThinkingPublications.com–This site features books, software, games, and assessment materials specially designed for children, adolescents, and adults with communication disorders.

www.toolboxofhope.com–This site is dedicated to the thousands of children who live with chronic, degenerative, and terminal illnesses.

www.uicisolutions.com–UICI Marketing provides information about the benefits available through the National Association For Self Employed (NASE), Alliance for Affordable Services (Alliance), and Americans for Financial Security (AFS).

www.viguide.com–This site contains information on many topics pertaining to parenting and teaching a child with visual impairments.

www.VisionConnection.org–This site is an interactive global internet portal for people who are partially sighted or blind, those who work with them, and families and friends who support them.

REFERENCES

Altshuler, I. (1948). A psychiatrist's experiences with music as a therapeutic agent. In D. Schullian & M. Schoen (Eds.), *Music in medicine.* New York: Henry Schuman, Inc.

American Music Therapy Association Member Sourcebook (2003). Elkins, A.G. (Ed.). Washington, DC: The American Music Therapy Association, Inc.

Boxhill, E. (1985). *Music therapy for the developmentally disabled.* Rockville, MD: Aspen Systems.

Boyd, Wm. D. (1978). *The use of field dependent music reinforcers to increase field independent behaviors.* Master's thesis. Denton, TX: Texas Woman's University.

Brotons, M., & Koger, S. (2000). The impact of music therapy on language functioning in dementia. *Journal of Music Therapy, 37*(3), 183.

Bruscia, K. (1989). *Defining music therapy.* Spring City, PA: Spring House Books.

Chesky, K., Michel, D., & Hummel, A. (1996). A pilot study of music and music vibration for pediatric pain management. *VI International MusicMedicine Symposium, Vol.2, Conference Abstracts.* San Antonio, TX: University of Texas Health Science Center at San Antonio.

Chesky, K., & Michel, D. (1996). Desensitization of central nociceptive neurons: Applications of music and music vibration in the surgical area. *VI International MusicMedicine Symposium, Vol.2, Conference Abstracts.* San Antonio, TX: University of Texas Health Science Center at San Antonio.

Chesky, K., Michel, D., & Hummel, A. (1997). Effects of music and music vibration with children in surgery. In J. Loewy (Ed.), *Music therapy and pediatric pain.* Cherry Hill, NJ: Jeffrey Books.

Chesky, K., & Michel, D. (1999). *Music and medicine: Medical problems of musicians.* Presentation at AMTA National Conference 1999. Washington, DC: American Music Therapy Association.

Clark, C., & Chadwick, D. (1979). *Clinically adapted instruments for the multiply handicapped.* Westford, MA: Modulations Co.

Chesky,K., Michel, D., & Hummel, A. (1997). Applications of music and music vibration with children in surgery. In J. Loewy (Ed.), *Music therapy and pediatric pain.* Cherry Hill, NJ: Jeffrey Books.

Coleman, K. (1995). *S.M.A.R.T. goals and objectives.* Personal communication.

Davis, G., White, T., & Hiemenz, M. (2002). Barriers to managing chronic pain of older adults with arthritis. *Journal of Nursing Scholarship, 2,* 121–125.

Education for All Handicapped Children Act of 1975. Public Law 94–142. Washington, DC: US 94th Congress, 6th Session, 20, USC 1401, Sec. 3 (6)(1).

Flavell, J.B. (1971). *The developmental psychology of Jean Piaget.* New York: Van Nostrand Reinhold.

Gaston, E. (1968). The development of man. In E. Gaston (Ed.), *Music in therapy* (pp. 10–13). New York: Macmillan,

Gionet, A., & Michel, D. (1995). *Music rherapy–An English translation of Lecourt, E. (1988) La Musicotherapie.* Published by the translators; distributed by MMB Music, Inc., St. Louis, MO. (Example of psychoanalytic theories applied to music therapy).

Glanze, W., Anderson, K., & Anderson, L. (Eds.). (1985). *Mosby Medical Encyclopedia (Rev. ed).* NY: Plume.

Hanser, S. (1999). *The new music therapist's handbook* (2nd ed.). MA: Berklee Press.

Hurt, C., Rice, R., McIntosh, G., & Thaut, M. (1998). Rhythmic auditory stimulation in gait training for patients with traumatic brain injury. *Journal of Music Therapy, 35* (4), 228.

Henrick, S., & Bock, J. (1964). Fiddler on the Roof. In D. Jacobs, *Who wrote that song?* Crozet, VA: Bellering, Inc.

Holmberg, T. (1996). T*he evolution of music therapy and its parallels to the published articles of Donald E. Michel.* Master's thesis. Denton, TX: Texas Woman's University.

Kitts, R. (1999). *Ethics for counselors.* Unpublished Presentation. Denton, TX: Denton Area Psychotherapy Association.

Lathom, W. (1981). Developmental CAMEO skills. In W. Lathom (Ed.), *Role of music therapy in the education of handicapped children and youth* (p. 18).Washington, DC: National Association for Music Therapy, Inc.

Lathom, W., & Eagle, C. (Eds.). (1984). *Music therapy for handicapped children (3 vols.).* Lawrence, KS: Messeraul.

Madsen, C., & Mears, W. (1965). The effect of sound on the tactile threshold of deaf subjects. *Journal of Music Therapy,* 64–68.

Masserman, J. (1966). *Therapy of personality disorders.* Dubuque, IA: Wm C. Brown.

Milieu Therapy (1950). *Guide to the order sheet–rev. 4,* MF–188 Topeka, KS: The Menninger Foundation.

Michel, D. (1950). The work of a hospital musician. *The Sinfonian.* Iowa State Teachers College: Phi Mu Alpha Fraternity of America.

Michel, D. (1959). Concluding report: A survey of three hundred seventy-five cases in music therapy. *Music Therapy 1959* (pp. 137-152). National Association for Music Therapy.

Michel, D. (1960). Presidential address: *Music Therapy 1961.* National Association for Music Therapy.

Michel, D. (1961). Music therapy in the southeastern region. *Music Therapy 1962.* National Association for Music Therapy.

Michel, D. (1965). Professional profile: The NAMT member and his clinical practices in music therapy. *Journal of Music Therapy, 11,* 124–129.

Michel, D., & Martin, D. (1970). Music and self-esteem: Research with disadvantaged problem boys in an elementary school. *Journal of Music Therapy, 7,* 124–127

Michel, D., & Farrell, D. (1973). Music and self-esteem: Disadvantaged problem boys in an all black elementary school. *Journal of Research in Music Education, 21,* 80–85

Michel, D. (1976). *Music therapy: An introduction, including music in special education.* Springfield, IL: Charles C Thomas.

Michel, D. (1985). *Music therapy: An introduction, including music in special education* (2nd ed.). Springfield, IL: Charles C Thomas.

Michel, D. (1985). Music therapy in a life-span developmental skills model. *Proceedings of the Eleventh National Conference of the Australian Music Therapy Association #5* (Keynote speech). Melbourne: Australian Music Therapy Association.

Michel, D., & Chesky, K. (1991). The Music Vibration Table (MVT): Developing a technology and conceptual model for pain relief. *Music Therapy Perspectives, 9,* 32–38.

Michel, D., & Rohrbacher, M. (1983). *Music Therapy Assessment Profile (MTAP) for Children, Ages 0–27 months.* Denton,TX.: Research Edition.

Michel, D. (1983). Music therapy in a resource class: Billy–a case history. In W. Lathom (Ed.), *Role of music therapy in the education of handicapped children and youth* (pp. 47–49). Washington, DC: National Association for Music Therapy.

Michel, D., & Jones, J. (1991). *Music for developing speech and language skills in children– A guide for parents and therapists.* St. Louis, MO: MMB Music.

Michel, D. (2000). An assessment of music therapy over the past fifty years and a vision of its future: My view (Special Feature). *Music Therapy Perspectives, 18,* 72–77.

Miller, S.E. (1982). *Music therapy for handicapped children: Speech impaired.* Washington, DC: National Association for Music Therapy.

Miller, S. (1999). Taylor's Four Way Test. In M. Kessel (Ed.), *Rotarians make a difference* (pp. 37–39). Dallas, TX: Dallas Offset.

Nelson, W. (1980). On the road again (song). In D. Jacobs (Ed.), *Who wrote that song.* Crozet, VA: Bellering.

Pinson, J. (1981). *There you are.* Unpublished poem.

Pinson, J. (1982). Case study: Mary. In D. Paul (Ed.), *Music therapy for handicapped children: Emotionally disturbed* (p. 33). Washington, DC: National Association for Music Therapy.

Pinson, J. (1989). *The music in my heart is for you.* Official Song of the American Music Therapy Association (AMTA)-Southwestern Region. Unpublished song.

Pinson, J. (1999). Light boards for bell choir ringers. In *Focus on participation: Alternate methods for hand bell choirs.* Dayton, OH: The American Guild of English Handbell Ringers.

Pinson, J., & Michel, D. (1999). Music therapy case study: *Qualitative assessment data made quantitative using the Music Therapy Assessment Profile* (Michel & Rohrbacher, 1982). Paper presented at the American Music Therapy Association Southwestern Regional Conference.

Pinson, J. (2000). *Clinical practicum lecture notes.* Unpublished.

Pribram, K. (1984). Meaning and music. *William W. Sears Distinguished Lecturer Series at the Annual Conference of the National Association for Music Therapy.* Washington, DC: National Association for Music Therapy.

Redmond, A. (1976). *The use of music training to facilitate right-left discrimination in young children.* Master's thesis. Denton, TX: Texas Woman's University.

Redmond, A. (1984). *The effect of music on fetal heart rate.* Unpublished doctoral dissertation. Denton, TX: Texas Woman's University.

Rider, M. (1997) *The rhythmic language of health and disease.* St. Louis, MO: MMB Music.

Sears, W. (1968). Processes in music therapy. In Gaston, E. (Ed.), *Music in therapy.* New York: Macmillan.

Selye, H. (1945). *The stress of life.* New York: McGraw-Hill.

Spielberger, C., Gorsuch, R., Lushene, R., Vagg, P., & Jacobs, G. (1980). *A manual for the State-Trait Anxiety Inventory Tests.* Palo Alto, CA: Counseling Psychologists Press.

Staum, M. (1983). Music and rhythmic stimuli in the rehabilitation of gait disorders. *Journal of Music Therapy, (20)* 2, 69.

Staum, M., & Brotons, M. (2000) The effect of music volume on the relaxation response. *Journal of Music Therapy, 37,* 1–22.

Subjective well-being (happiness) (2001). In N. Eddington & R. Shuman (Eds.), *Continuing education for licensed professional counselors and licensed family and marriage therapists.* Austin, TX: Department of Continuing Psychology Education.

Summer, L. (1992). *Guided imagery and music in the institutional setting.* St.Louis, MO: MMB Music.

Summer, L. (1996). *Music: the new age elixir.* Amsterdam, NY: Prometheous Books.

Thaut, M. (1990). Neuropsychological processes in music perception and their relevance in music therapy. In R. Unkefer (Ed.), *Music therapy in the treatment of adults with mental disorders* (pp. 3–32). New York: Schirmer.

Thaut, M. (2000). *A scientific model of music in therapy and medicine.* IMR Press: The University of Texas at San Antonio. St. Louis: MMB Music.

INDEX